Culture and Power in Traditional Siamese Government

T0340674

CONTENTS

ACKNOWLEDGMENTS

I have benefited in this work from the generous assistance of the Thailand–United States Educational Foundation (Fulbright), the Thaikhadi Research Institute at Thammasat University, and the staffs of the National Research Council of Thailand, the Thai National Archives, the Thai National Library, and the Siam Society. Victor Magagna, Tracy Strong, Peter Gourevitch, Roy D'Andrade, F. G. Bailey, Katherine Underwood, Melissa Miller, Michael Montesano, Thongchai Winichakul, and David Wyatt have all read the manuscript, and I have benefited immensely from their comments. I also wish to thank Deborah Homsher, Erick White, and Rattawut Lapcharoensap for their outstanding editorial assistance. Any errors or omissions are, of course, the responsibility of the author.

PREFACE

The goal of this essay is to provide an interpretation of political life in nineteenth-century Siam. I seek to elucidate the way people thought about power and politics and to link those ways of thinking with the structure of the political system. I want to show how that system appeared reasonable and orderly to those who lived with it and tried to accomplish their goals within it. Contrary to European contemporaries and later scholars, who have seen chaos and disorder in the early Bangkok period polity, I argue that it was in fact ordered and effective in terms of the local political culture, although it was eventually undermined by changing circumstances.

This essay began as a portion of my dissertation. I originally set out to write about the remarkable transformation of Siamese politics in the reign of King Chulalongkorn as a case of intentional cultural change. In my dissertation I was interested in the relationship between culture, cognition, and reason in explaining political behavior. These interests are reflected in the methodological assumptions of this book, and especially in the introduction and conclusion.

However, it soon became apparent that I had to deal with a prior historiographical issue. Chulalongkorn's transformation of political life in Siam seemed a little too remarkable as it was portrayed in the existing historiography. Most accounts of the old system of government claimed that it had been inefficient and corrupt, and that the king's power had been so circumscribed as to make him helpless to control events outside—or even inside—the capital. This was held to be the case until King Chulalongkorn burst asunder the old order and replaced it with the very highly centralized regime which, in its basic pattern, continues to characterize Thai politics today.

It rapidly became apparent to me that something was wrong with the way royal power in the old system had been characterized. Without detracting from Chulalongkorn's admittedly remarkable accomplishments, it simply was not possible that he had done so much with so little. He must have had some initial resources to start with. The traditional account, which posited kings who had no control over provincial government and who were severely circumscribed in the capital, made the reform process much too magical. In addition to the original task of understanding the changes in Siamese political life in the latter part of the Fifth Reign, I therefore had to add the task of revising my interpretation of the old Siamese system of government. The essay that follows is meant to satisfy the latter goal by constructing an ideal type of early Bangkok period government and politics.

My focus here is primarily on the Fourth and early Fifth Reigns. This reflects both my initial interest in the historical conditions at the time King Chulalongkorn ascended the throne in 1868 and the materials to which I had access when conducting my research. I would argue, however, that many of the principles I discuss apply equally well to the first three reigns of the early Bangkok period and might provide insights into earlier periods.

In transliterating from Thai, I have generally followed the system employed in Lucien Hanks' *Rice and Man*, on the grounds that it is the most intuitive system available for speakers of English who do not know Thai. The only exception is that I have substituted *-eu* for Hanks' *-y*. Other exceptions include commonly known names (eg. Nakhon Si Thammarat instead of Nakhaun Si Thamarat or Chulalongkorn instead of Culacaumklaw), or where the expressed preference of a person is known to me (as in the transliteration and English translation of the titles of Thai theses).

Chapter 1

INTRODUCTION

The literature on pre-modern Siamese government emphasizes its inefficiency, and in particular the lack of central government control over provincial centers of power. H. G. Quaritch Wales, for instance, repeatedly refers to Siamese government as "degenerate" and "decadent." He characterizes the Siamese as

> a people which, while accepting and applying elaborate administrative methods, largely borrowed or adopted from more advanced civilizations, had little understanding of the underlying principles, and no definitely expressed conception of the theory of government or the social order.[1]

According to Quaritch Wales the government could only be restored to full efficiency by strong monarchs and unsettled conditions: " . . . weak kings and long periods of peace undermined the power of the government to such an extent that it could only be restored by the most able monarchs, and then only temporarily."[2]

The same emphasis on the rejuvenating and centralizing effects of crisis recurs in Akin Rabibhadana's classic *The Organization of Thai Society in the Early Bangkok Period*. Akin also sees long periods of peace as undermining the king's control over manpower by promoting the growth of informal clientage arrangements. The system was therefore at its most efficient immediately following some catastrophe that forced the king to take extraordinary measures, reconstituting an official hierarchy stripped of such informal arrangements. In peace "the formal hierarchy of ranks ceased to correlate with the actual distribution of power," weakening the kingdom. In this peril, paradoxically, lay the seeds of strength: " . . . if attacks came at such a time from a neighboring land, they would be hard to resist. A major defeat, such as the loss of the capital, would, however, allow the emergence of a new hierarchy without the informal clientships, and this gave strength to the king and the kingdom."[3] Peace allowed an extensive network of subordinates to grow up between the king and his subjects, thereby limiting the king's power.

---

[1] H. G. Quaritch Wales, *Ancient Siamese Government and Administration* (New York: Paragon, 1965 [1934]), p. 1. Quaritch Wales's standard for decadence is the Siamese deviation from Khmer models of government. He appears to be referring to the late Ayuthaya and early Bangkok periods.

[2] Ibid., p. 248.

[3] Akin Rabibhadana, *The Organization of Thai Society in the Early Bangkok Period, 1782-1873* (Ithaca: Cornell Southeast Asia Program, 1969), p. 183. Akin sees this as a long-term cycle in Thai history, of which the events of the Bangkok period are only one example.

The Thai literature on the early Bangkok period similarly emphasizes the manner in which subordinates limited the power of the king.[4] Piyachat Pitawan even argues that there was a total collapse of royal authority in the early part of King Chulalongkorn's reign, as the central government lost all control over politics at the local level.[5]

Thai kings themselves seem to have been frustrated by their lack of power, and they occasionally experimented with new policies designed to increase their control over local officials.[6] The most famous such innovator, King Chulalongkorn, left us a detailed list of his frustrations with the old system, particularly regarding issues of legal jurisdiction and tax collection.[7]

Yet the very success of Chulalongkorn's reform makes this interpretation of Siamese politics problematic. Chulalongkorn, who began his reign as one of the weakest of the supposedly weak Thai kings, was able to muster the resources to support a radical reform program. This reform, which amounted to a revolution from above, was so effective that even those whose interests were most directly effected barely protested. Although the reform faced political obstacles and delays, it went far more smoothly than comparable state-building projects in Europe or Japan. How could the weakest of a weak line have achieved this coup?

While recent scholarship has tended to characterize traditional Thai kings as comparatively helpless, the historical record contradicts this. Many contemporary European observers regarded the Thai king as an absolute monarch whose every whim was law. Crawfurd, for instance, wrote that the monarchy was "as complete an example of despotic power vested in one man as can well be imagined," an opinion with which the more tolerant Bowring concurred.[8] This view was due in part to the absolute authority of the king to make and unmake law, which Europeans identified as a hallmark of "oriental despotism."

Some modern historians have also pointed out that the supposedly weak monarch actually had considerable authority some distance from the capital. Terwiel, for instance, writes that one of his "unexpected findings has been the discovery of the

---

[4] See for instance อัญชลี สุสายัณห์, "ความเปลี่ยนแปลงของระบบไพร่และผลกระทบต่อสังคมไทยใน รัชสมัยพระบาทสมเด็จพระจุลจอมเกล้าเจ้าอยู่หัว" [Anchalee Susayanha, "Changes of the Phrai System and Their Effects on Thai Society in the Reign of King Chulalongkorn"] (MA Thesis in History, Chulalongkorn University, BE 2524), pp. 31-2.

[5] ปิยะฉัตร ปิตะวรรณ, *ระบบไพร่ในสังคมไทย พศ ๒๔๑๑ – ๒๔๕๓* [Piyachat Pitawan, *The Phrai System in Thai Society BE 2411 – 2453*] (Bangkok: Thammasat University Press, BE 2526), p. 67.

[6] For instance จดหมายเหตุ ร. ๔ ๑๒๒๐/๕๕.

[7] "พระราชดำรัสในพระบาทสมเด็จพระจุลจอมเกล้าเจ้าอยู่หัวทรงแถลงพระบรมราชาธิบายแก้ไขการปก- ครองแผ่นดิน" ["Proclamation of King Chulalongkorn Explaining the Improvements in the Administration of the Kingdom"] in ชัยอนันต์ สมุทวณิช และ ขัตติยา กรรณสูต รวบรวม, *เอกสาร การเมืองการปกครองไทย (พศ ๒๔๑๗ – ๒๔๗๗)* [Chai-anan Samudavanija and Khatthiya Kansut, ed., *Thai Political and Administrative Documents (BE 2417 – 2477)*] (Bangkok: Social Science Association of Thailand, BE 2532), pp. 72-99.

[8] John Crawfurd, *The Crawfurd Papers* (Bangkok: Vajiranana National Library, 1915), p. 121; and John Bowring, *The Kingdom and People of Siam*, vol. I (New York: Oxford University Press, 1969), pp. 93, 170.

size and efficiency of the nineteenth-century government apparatus—direct Bangkok influence reached into regions hundreds of kilometers and several days distant."[9] Wilson has argued that Bangkok was quite successful at controlling subordinate towns and even distant tributaries.[10]

There is one point on which all parties agree, however: the pre-modern Siamese government was organized around the control of people rather than land or money. In the pre-modern context, where land was abundant and labor was scarce, people were the most valuable resource. Control over people was the source and indicator of wealth and power.[11]

This means that the efficiency of pre-modern Siamese government cannot be judged by modern standards. Early Bangkok period Siamese officials were not trying to accomplish the same goals as twentieth-century bureaucrats. They were not trying to create a modern state characterized by domination of territory, bureaucratic efficiency, or a monopoly of the use of violence; they were trying to control manpower using traditional, time-tested techniques. To judge the system by other standards naturally makes it appear wanting. King Chulalongkorn's own criticism of the old system is not surprising, as he was trying to change it to make it more like a modern state on the European colonial model. His proclamations explaining and justifying the changes he made are the last place one should look for a sympathetic and unbiased reading of the old system.[12]

I will argue that for most of the early Bangkok period, Siamese government was quite effective on its own terms. Kings had supreme authority, as the king was seen as the most meritorious person in the kingdom and stood at the pinnacle of the social order in what was a very hierarchical system. Furthermore, kings traditionally had a great deal of military power and could enforce their will anywhere in the kingdom. However, given the logic of the old system and the goals that kings pursued, it was actually advantageous for the monarch to *choose* to give local level officials a great

---

[9] B. J. Terwiel, *Through Traveller's Eyes: An Approach to Nineteenth-Century Thai History* (Bangkok: Duang Komol, 1989), p. 251.

[10] Constance Wilson, "State and Society in the Reign of King Mongkut, 1851-1868: Thailand on the eve of Modernization" (PhD Dissertation, Cornell University, 1970), p. 448.

[11] This is recognized by virtually all authors working on pre-modern Siam. See for instance Quaritch Wales, *Ancient Siamese Government*, pp. 9-10, 46, and 97; Akin, *Organization of Thai Society*, pp. 16, 19, and 77; Wilson, "State and Society," p. 91; อัญชลี, "ระบบไพร่" [Anchalee, "Phrai System"], pp. 25-9; ปิยะฉัตร, ระบบไพร่ [Piyachat, *Phrai System*], pp. 20, 67; บุญรอด แก้วกันหา, "การเก็บส่วยในสมัยรัตนโกสินทร์ตอนต้น (พศ ๒๓๒๕ – ๒๔๑๑)" [Boonrod Keawkanha, "The Collection of Suay During the Early Ratanakosin Period (AD 1782–1868)"] (MA Thesis in History, Chulalongkorn University, BE 2518), p. 44; and นันทิยา สว่างวุฒิธรรม, "การควบคุมกำลังคนในสมัยรัตนโกสินทร์ก่อนการจัดการเกณฑ์ทหาร (พ.ศ. ๒๓๒๕ – ๒๔๔๘)," [Nuntiya Swangvudthitham, "The Control of Manpower During the Bangkok Period Prior to the Introduction of Modern Conscription (BE 2325-2448)"] (MA Thesis in History, Chulalongkorn University, BE 2525), p. 200.

[12] On this point see also Hong Lysa, *Thailand in the Nineteenth Century: Evolution of Economy and Society* (Singapore: Institute of Southeast Asian Studies, 1984), p. 5. As discussed in Chapter Five below, the social and economic conditions supporting the system were beginning to erode, especially in the central plains, by the Fifth Reign.

deal of autonomy. Kings were not satisfied with the institutions and strategies they had inherited from their predecessors, and sometimes they experimented with alternatives. They would have preferred a more centralized system that gave them more direct control over their subjects. However, they had to work within constraints that forced them to retain the structure of the system as it existed. Understanding the nature of these constraints and the logic of the system requires a sympathetic reconstruction of how the people operating within it thought about power and politics. With such a reconstruction we can appreciate how monarchs who might appear weak to modern observers were nevertheless still able to muster the resources necessary for a revolution from above.

CULTURE AND CHOICE

In this study I attempt to understand the political organization of early Bangkok period Siam as a function of culture and choice.[13] The conception of culture I employ is drawn from cognitive anthropology.[14] The fundamental insight of cognitive anthropology is that people who share a culture share conceptual resources that they use to understand and interpret the world. These resources are called concepts or schemata.

Schemata are processes of pattern recognition that enable people to understand sensory inputs as representing particular objects or events. Schemata are linked, so that a variety of other schemata are drawn into a single act of recognition. For instance, in recognizing a person, various schemata for wealth, class, race, gender, and so on are simultaneously tapped. These in turn connect to other schemata governing proper patterns of interaction with such a person. They also connect to higher-level schemata, which provide explanations for how to recognize such people, how to interact with them properly, and so on. Some of these modes of behavior we may recognize as legitimate, as part of the way things ought to be. Others we may recognize as illegitimate, part of the way things are, even though they should not be that way. If we cannot recognize behavior as being consistent with any set of schemata, it is likely to seem troubling or puzzling to us; if sufficiently distant from any pattern of behavior we know, we might dismiss it as bizarre or irrational.

Schemata are hierarchically linked, providing goals and strategies for enacting them.[15] If I want to achieve political power, for instance, I will follow the patterns of behavior I have learned to recognize as effective for attaining that end. In twentieth-century America this means that I might try to win nomination for office under one of the major party labels. This may involve means that are recognized as legitimate — e.g., fund-raising and campaign work. These actions invoke still more basic schemata; for instance, to compose campaign literature I will draw on schemata for language use, for operating my computer, for striking keys on a keyboard, etc. It may also involve schemata for means that are considered illegitimate, such as soliciting

---

[13] For a fuller discussion of these issues, see Neil A. Englehart, "Culture, Choice and Change in Thailand in the Reign of King Chulalongkorn, 1868-1910" (PhD Dissertation, University of California, San Diego, 1996), pp. 29-63.

[14] For an introduction to the field, see Roy D'Andrade, *The Development of Cognitive Anthropology* (New York: Cambridge University Press, 1995).

[15] Roy D'Andrade and Claudia Strauss, eds., *Human Motives and Cultural Models* (New York: Cambridge University Press, 1992).

illegal campaign contributions, writing unfair attack ads, and so on. There are culturally shared schemata for both good and ill.

Many schemata seem obvious and trivial. Most never attract our conscious attention. As we operate in our lives, they continually supply commonsense notions about how the world works, ideas we take for granted. However, schemata vary culturally. The ordinary, common sense schemata of one culture may make no sense in another. To understand the behavior of people in another culture, we need to understand the schemata with which they are operating. These may include schemata that they take for granted and do not themselves notice in operation.[16] It also means that we must take care not to apply our own "common sense" notions and judgments to the behavior of people in other cultures, for in so doing we risk misinterpreting that behavior through our own schemata.

Each higher-level schema acts as a goal, with lower-level schemata acting as means for achieving that end. In Siam, for instance, political power was a function of the number of followers one had, and achieving the goal of having power therefore entailed acquiring followers. The political culture consequently included schemata for achieving this end, e.g. by reducing the tax burden on one's clients. This then became a subsidiary goal, to which culturally learned methods might be applied, and so on.

The relationship between these subsidiary goals is instrumental, and therefore not stable. People are constantly looking for new and better ways to achieve their goals. They innovate, and they look for ideas to borrow from others. As these innovations spread, culture changes. Thus, I will argue below that King Chulalongkorn was exposed to European ideas about politics through his unusual education, and in these ideas he found new ways to deal with the problems he faced. As he applied these new solutions, Siamese political culture was changed.[17]

People often have to choose between goals or between multiple strategies available for reaching the same goal. They also are often dissatisfied with the choices they have, and so they try to come up with innovative solutions to the problems confronting them. In all these cases, there is an irreducible element of creativity and choice in people's behavior, which must be taken into account in explaining any given set of behaviors. Thus, below I discuss both culture—in particular the way political power was understood—and the choices people made based on the interests and incentives generated by culturally shared schemata. Individuals acted in accordance with their interests, but they could do so only because they had culturally acquired ways to think about what their interests were, what goals would best serve those interests, and what strategies were available for achieving those goals.

---

[16] This taken-for-granted quality that underlies much knowledge gained through experience, rather than schooling, is similar to what Bourdieu terms "doxa." See Pierre Bourdieu, *Outline of a Theory of Practice*, trans. Richard Nice (New York: Cambridge University Press, 1977), p. 164. On the relationship between Bourdieu and cognitive anthropology, see Claudia Strauss and Naomi Quinn, *A Cognitive Theory of Cultural Meaning* (New York: Cambridge University Press, 1997), pp. 44-7.

[17] This is true not just of novel problems, but also of problems generated within a culture. See for instance Thomas Metzger, *Escape from Predicament: Neo-Confucianism and China's Evolving Political Culture* (New York: Columbia University Press, 1977), in which the author argues that Chinese intellectuals perceived in certain Western philosophies solutions to long-standing problems in Neo-Confucian thought.

Following this method I hope to avoid both the Scylla of cultural reductionism and the Charybdis of ethnocentric assumptions about the nature of rationality.

IDEAL TYPES

My goal in the next two chapters is to develop an ideal type of early Bangkok period Siamese government that elucidates the concepts underlying political life. In doing so, I am trying to show how people working within traditional Siamese political culture could reasonably act in the ways indicated by the historical record. In this, my account differs from others that emphasize chaos and disorder in politics, but do not give adequate attention to the model of political order from which that chaos was supposed to have deviated.

An ideal type is a logically consistent account of a social phenomenon designed to make that phenomenon more tractable for empirical research. It should reveal how actions that appear strange or irrational actually have a certain logical consistency from the point of view of the actors. Ideal types are analytical constructs, not pure accounts of reality. Weber refers to them as "utopias," writing that ". . . in its conceptual purity, this mental construct cannot be found empirically anywhere in reality."[18] Its utility is in providing analytic clarity.

The real world is, of course, not so tidy. People get confused, act irrationally, or become victims of abnormal circumstances. Crises develop, harvests fail, personalities conflict, and people act foolishly. Ideal types do not attempt to account for these sorts of events or problems. Instead, they aim to cut through the confusion such events generate, to find a core of consistency that is accessible to deeper understanding. As Weber puts it, an ideal type "has the merit of clear understandability and lack of ambiguity. By comparison with this it is possible to understand the ways in which actual action is influenced by irrational factors of all sorts."[19]

Ideal types are not necessarily articulated clearly in the mind of any individual subject.

> Those "ideas" which govern the behavior of the population in a certain epoch i.e., which are concretely influential in determining their conduct can, if a somewhat complicated construct is involved, be formulated precisely only in the form of an ideal type, since empirically it exists in the minds of an indefinite and constantly changing mass of individuals and assumes in their minds the most multifarious nuances of form and content, clarity and meaning.[20]

The people who participated in Siamese politics each had his or her own perspective, and probably few if any thought about the structure of the system as a whole. The structure elucidated below is my analysis of the principles by which most people seem to have conducted political life, based on the evidence provided by their behavior.

---

[18] Max Weber, *The Methodology of the Social Sciences*, trans. and ed. Edward Shils and Henry Finch (New York: The Free Press, 1949), p. 90.

[19] Max Weber, *Economy and Society*, vol. 1, ed. Guenther Ross and Claus Wittich (Berkeley: University of California Press, 1978), p. 6.

[20] Weber, *Methodology of the Social Sciences*, pp. 95-6.

There is a final caveat. This method of presenting a political system in the form of an ideal type has the drawback of making that system appear static. The pre-modern Siamese government was in fact extremely dynamic, changing over time in response to conflict, crises, and innovations. The basic system was created by the quasi-bureaucratic reforms of King Trailok of Ayuthaya in the fifteenth century. The system continued to evolve throughout the Ayuthaya period. A major innovation took place in the Thonburi period when King Taksin (r. 1767-1782) introduced the practice of tattooing all commoners with the name of their lord. Further adjustments took place in the early Bangkok period, including King Rama I's (r. 1782-1809) modification of corvée service requirements. The rate of change accelerated from the reign of King Rama III (r. 1824-1851) on, as economic and social change began to undermine the conditions that had sustained the political system. Particularly important watersheds were passed in 1826 and 1856, in response to treaties with the British.

Despite these changes, however, the system of government outlined below remained the basic model for Siamese politics until the administrative changes introduced by King Chulalongkorn in the late 1880s and 1890s. The static nature of the ideal type is not meant to deny historical change, but rather to emphasize and clarify the basic model of politics that persisted from the rehabilitation of the kingdom after the Burmese invasions in the 1760s, into the reign of King Chulalongkorn.

THE PLAN OF THE BOOK

Having dealt with preliminary theoretical issues in this chapter, I move on to an empirical account of Siamese government in the early Bangkok period (1782-1910) in the following four chapters. Chapter Two is an account of the social context of the early Bangkok period kingdom, emphasizing the schemata that formed the foundation of Siamese political culture. Chapter Three is a description of the political institutions of the kingdom at the local level. These grassroots institutions formed the building blocks of provincial and central government institutions, discussed in Chapter Four. The ideal type of Siamese government advanced in Chapters Three and Four presents an overly static impression of the polity. Chapter Five is intended to correct this with a brief narrative of important changes in the political structure of this kingdom during this period. Chapter Five concludes with an account of the reforms of King Chulalongkorn that ended the old system of government and created a modern state. Chapter Six concludes the book by briefly comparing state formation in Siam with similar attempts in Burma and Japan. It then concludes with a reprise of the major theoretical points of the book: the significance and relationships between culture, choice, and power.

Chapter 2

SOCIAL AND CULTURAL CONTEXT

The political culture of the early Bangkok period developed in a particular physical and cultural environment. The geography and climate of the kingdom set physical limits for the institutions that were feasible. Culturally shared schemata for understanding political life were based on broader concepts of merit and hierarchy through which social life was interpreted. These concepts led individuals to participate in a system of clientage relations that formed the foundation of the political system. The court employed these schemata in advancing a theory of Buddhist kingship that emphasized the superiority of the monarchy. However, it is crucial to recognize that this was only one strand of a more complex cultural phenomenon, for the culture also provided ways for thinking about evading or resisting royal power.

THE PHYSICAL AND CULTURAL ENVIRONMENT OF THE EARLY BANGKOK PERIOD

In the early nineteenth century, Siam was blessed with abundant and fertile land and a low population density. Food was relatively easy to grow, especially in the Caophraya river flood plain. There farming did not require the extensive social coordination required within villages in many other parts of the world.[1] A family

---

[1] Pre-modern Thai villages took the form of houses scattered along waterways, rather than gathered into clusters, a pattern that provides evidence that agriculture there did not require much organized cooperation between farmers. In other parts of the kingdom social coordination might have been more important, particularly in those places where it was necessary to build and maintain irrigation works. In those areas villages did cluster. See คมเนตร ญาณโสภณ, "อำนาจท้องถิ่นแบบจารีตและผลกระทบจากการเปลี่ยนแปลงการปกครองท้องถิ่นในยุคเทศาภิบาล" [Khomnet Yansophon, "Traditional Local Power and the Impact of the Change of Local Administration in the Thesaphiban Period"] (MA Thesis in the Faculty of Arts, Thammasat University, BE 2534), Chapter 1; and Joseph Ingersoll, "Merit and Identity in Village Thailand," in *Change and Persistence in Thai Society: Essays in Honor of Lauriston Sharp*, ed. G. William Skinner and A. Thomas Kirsch (Ithaca: Cornell University Press, 1975), p. 222. There was little of the intense mutual dependence we see in climates where agriculture required extensive cooperation, as described for instance in Victor V. Magagna, *Communities of Grain: Rural Rebellion in Comparative Perspective* (Ithaca: Cornell University Press, 1991).

could typically grow enough rice to support itself and had little reason to grow more. Because of the low population density, there was little competition for land.

In this idyllic material setting, the primary commodity in short supply was labor, not for economic ends, but for political and religious ones.[2] People were needed to staff and supply armies, to build fortifications and temples, to prepare and attend the cremation of nobles, to form retinues for officials, and to supply luxury goods to the capital. Numerous followers became the premium marker of status and power for leaders.[3]

The arrangement of social groups into hierarchies of leaders and followers was considered a normal and natural part of life in old Siam, where a fundamental inequality between individuals was assumed, and political and social patterns were constructed on the basis of that assumption. This is still reflected today in the language, which has elaborate vocabularies for marking the differences between people,[4] and in social customs which require that people be able to place each other as superior or inferior in order to interact with civility.[5] These schemata were also reflected in political and religious practices.[6]

Thai children in the nineteenth century were taught from birth to expect and respect hierarchy. From early childhood people were trained to obey superiors, use deferential language, and expect protection from the powerful. Children were taught the linguistic, sartorial, and organizational cues used to determine the status of others and to display one's own status. Experience with the local temple, and with government operations such as corvée (taxation in the form of unpaid labor), taught

---

[2] Lauriston Sharp and Lucien M. Hanks, *Bang Chan: Social History of a Rural Community in Thailand* (Ithaca: Cornell University Press, 1978), p. 45. There was little money in circulation at the beginning of the Bangkok period; cowry shells were still being used as currency in some areas. The economy seems to have monetarized steadily over the course of the Bangkok period, however. See Junko Koizumi, "The Commutation of *Suai* from Northeast Thailand in the Middle of the Nineteenth Century," *Journal of Southeast Asian Studies* 23,2 (1992): 276-307.

[3] ปิยะฉัตร ปิตะวรรณ, *ระบบไพร่ในสังคมไทย พศ ๒๔๑๑ - ๒๔๕๓* [Piyachat Pitawan, *The Phrai System in Thai Society BE 2411 - 2453*] (Bangkok: Thammasat University Press, BE 2526), p. 67.

[4] "Thai linguistic structure is such that it is impossible to address a person without referring to social status." Hans-Dieter Bechstedt, "Identity and Authority in Thailand," in *National Identity and Its Defenders: Thailand 1939-1989*, ed. Craig J. Reynolds (Chiang Mai: Silkworm Books, 1991), p. 304. Jeremy Kemp notes that the structure and use of Thai kin terms produces "maximum differentiation among kin with whom one is likely to have the most frequent and personally significant contact." See Jeremy Kemp, "The Manipulation of Personal Relationships: From Kinship to Patron-Clientage," in *Strategies and Structures in Thai Society*, ed. Han ten Brummelhuis and Jeremy Kemp (Amsterdam: Antropologisch-Sociologisch Centrum, Universiteit van Amsterdam, #31 Publikatieserie Vakgroep Zuid-en Zuidoest-Azie, 1984), p. 58. Kemp argues that the Thai use of fictive kinship, which is extensive, can represent an attempt at social manipulation since it requires people to be identified with non-voluntary roles.

[5] "It is worth emphasizing that this is a system in which, conceptually speaking, there are no equals," writes Kemp. See Kemp, "The Manipulation of Personal Relationships," p. 58. Even identical twins will refer to each other as elder or younger sibling (*phi* or *naung*) depending on which exited the birth canal first.

[6] The Buddhist clergy, the Sangha, is in theory one of the most egalitarian institutions in Thailand, but even so there is a carefully regulated hierarchy of official status, and even when the monks go out to beg for food in the morning the eldest monk by tradition is the first in the line.

respect for authority and hierarchy.[7] Almost all education in the old system occurred in temple schools,[8] where local monks taught children reading and the fundamentals of Buddhist practice. These lessons reinforced a belief in the legitimacy and normality of status distinctions and connected them to the idea of karma.

The concept of karma crystallizes many of the habits and concepts associated with status and proper social behavior, both then and today. Karma accounts for all those parts of one's fate outside of one's control: sex, social status, wealth, opportunity, talent, and luck. The concept is central to Thai Buddhism and spans regional and class variations in practice and belief.[9]

Thai Buddhism teaches that one's position and success in this life is the result of karma.[10] Those who have better karma—who have accumulated more merit—are superior to others who do not have such good karma. "Beings," says the Buddha in a well-known Pali text, "have each their own Karma, are inheritors of Karma, belong to the tribe of their Karma, have each their Karma as their protecting overlord. It is Karma that divides them up into low and high and like divisions."[11] In this view, differences between people are seen to be inherent. The Thai Buddhist solution to the problem of theodicy is thus the core of the religion: people suffer because of their own past actions. Karma is the automatic and perfect working of cosmic justice.

The average Thai Buddhist does not subscribe to the elegant philosophical system generally taught by scholars of Buddhism in the West. The latter holds that Buddhists believe that life is suffering, that desire is the cause of suffering, and that

---

[7] Bechstedt, "Identity and Authority." Schooling accomplishes many of the same ends today.

[8] วุฒิชัย มูลศิลป์, *การปฏิรูปการศึกษาในสมัยพระบาทสมเด็จพระจุลจอมเกล้าเจ้าอยู่หัว* [Wutichai Munsin, *The Reformation of Education in the Reign of King Chulalongkorn*] (Bangkok: Thai Wattana Panich, BE 2529), p. 9.

[9] Kamala Tiyavanich, *Forest Recollections: Wandering Monks in Twentieth-Century Thailand* (Honolulu: University of Hawai'i Press, 1997), Chapters 1 and 2. Indeed, it serves a similar function in many non-Thai versions of Buddhism. See for instance Nicola Tannenbaum's analysis of Shan religion, in *Who Can Compete Against the World?: Power-Protection and Buddhism in Shan Worldview* (Ann Arbor: Association for Asian Studies, 1995); and Manning Nash, *The Golden Road to Modernity: Village Life in Contemporary Burma* (New York: John Wiley, 1965), on Burma. I am not arguing that Buddhism causes Thais to have these ideas, but rather that the practice of Buddhism in Thailand draws on these schemata, which many Thais describe in Buddhist terms. Similar notions can be found in non-Buddhist cultures in Southeast Asia as well. See for instance Benedict Anderson's account of Java. Benedict Anderson, "The Idea of Power in Javanese Culture," in *Language and Power: Exploring Political Cultures in Indonesia* (Ithaca: Cornell University Press, 1990), pp. 17-77.

[10] The following discussion of Thai Buddhism draws on Jane Bunnag, *Buddhist Monk, Buddhist Layman: A Study of Urban Monastic Organization in Central Thailand* (New York: Cambridge University Press, 1973); B. J. Terwiel, *Monks and Magic: An Analysis of Religious Ceremonies in Central Thailand* (Lund: Scandinavian Institute of Asian Studies, 1975), p. 220; Yoneo Ishii, *Sangha, State and Society: Thai Buddhism in History*, trans. Peter Hawkes (Honolulu: University of Hawai'i Press, 1986); Stanley Jeyaraja Tambiah, *The Buddhist Saints of the Forest and the Cult of Amulets: A Study in Charisma, Hagiography, Sectarianism, and Millennial Buddhism* (New York: Cambridge University Press, 1984); Stanley Jeyaraja Tambiah, *Buddhism and the Spirit Cults in North-east Thailand* (New York: Cambridge University Press, 1970); and Stanley Jeyaraja Tambiah, *World Conqueror and World Renouncer: A Study of Buddhism and Polity in Thailand Against a Historical Background* (New York: Cambridge University Press, 1976); as well as my own observations.

[11] T. W. Rhys Davids, trans., *The Questions of King Milinda*, vol. I (Delhi: Motital Banarsidass, 1975 [1890]), p. 101.

desire can only be eliminated by engaging in practices which help one eliminate all the effects of actions in past lives (karma, both good and bad), so that they can achieve nirvana (no-existence), breaking the cycle of rebirth. Few Thais would identify extinction as the goal of their religious practice; most simply want to make merit in order to accumulate good karma, so that they will have a more comfortable rebirth in the future.[12] In Thai popular practice even the Four Noble Truths are sometimes transformed into a generic magical formula to ward off bad luck.

Most Thais wish to be reborn as a superior person, more capable and lucky. People with superior birth have more money and power, and are believed to be intrinsically more capable, effective, and lucky than those with inferior births. If an inferior wants to get something done in this life, the rational thing for that person to do is to find a superior who will assist him in achieving those things the inferior is incapable of attaining independently.[13]

Westerners might assume that such inequality must be onerous to the inferiors, and therefore resented. For people operating with this set of schemata, that is not necessarily the case. The inferior generally considers himself or herself to be inferior and voluntarily seeks a superior. Furthermore, the inferior is free to look for another superior, just as the superior is free to deny help to inferiors.[14]

Both superior and inferior get something valuable out of this relationship, and they both ought to recognize this; it is in the self-interest of superiors to fulfill their obligation to help their inferiors, just as it is in the inferior's interest to seek help. One cannot be a superior if one has driven off or abandoned all of one's followers.

The cognitive and self-interested components of the relationship are inseparable:

> In the West we consider a reciprocal exchange possible only between cooperating equals; inequality of station seems to constrain us. The Thai, however, because they assume symbiosis to form the basis of reciprocity, deem an inequality to be essential. . . . Americans are encouraged to feel safe by relying on themselves to attain their goals and to sense a risk when depending on others, but the Thai reverse the paradigm, feeling more secure when they have the backing of a strong patron.[15]

If merit does not result in high birth, according to these schemata it will at least be reflected in outstanding abilities and produce great achievements. Poor men with ability might become powerful gangsters, or *nakleng*. In the nineteenth century these men would gather followers around them, and might raid other villages, mostly for cattle, or rob passers-by on the road. Often they were associated with particular villages, and within those villages they would be recognized as local heroes, for they helped mount defenses against the raids initiated by other villages. Since they used violence, however, the actions of these men were considered sinful. Often in later life

---

[12] Terwiel, *Monks and Magic*, p. 220. See also Bunnag, *Buddhist Monk, Buddhist Layman*, p. 186.

[13] Lucien Hanks, "Merit and Power in the Thai Social System," in *Modern Thai Politics: From Village to Nation*, ed. Clark P. Neher (Cambridge, MA: Schenkman, 1976), p. 111.

[14] For this reason the ingratitude of others is a constant sore spot in Thai social relations, much as the infringement of rights is in America.

[15] Lucien Hanks, *Rice and Man: Agricultural Ecology in Southeast Asia* (Chicago: Aldive-Atherton, 1972), pp. 84, 103. It should also be noted that virtually everyone can enjoy superior status relative to someone else, as a parent or elder sibling, restaurant patron, or even by giving money to beggars, who constitute a sort of class of professional freelance inferiors.

they would settle down and become powerful and influential members of the village, or even village headmen (*phu yai ban*). Their illegally acquired wealth enabled them to engage in numerous merit-making activities which, they hoped, would more than compensate for sins committed in their youth.[16]

On the other hand, one's merit may support great achievement, but run out in the end. A classic example of this is the life of King Taksin, who recreated the Siamese state in the eighteenth century after it was destroyed by internal decay and the sacking of the capital by the Burmese. Having arisen from a relatively low status, Taksin reconstituted the entire kingdom, only to go mad and be deposed in a palace coup by nobles he had himself appointed. "The tragedy of King Taksin . . . is interpreted as meaning the King's *bun* [merit] was exhausted [*sinbun*]. Facing his executioners Taksin is reported to have said 'since my *bun* is exhausted, I have arrived now at my death.'"[17]

Kings are always attributed a very high degree of merit because of their high birth, and a king is generally thought to be the most meritorious person in the kingdom. This provides an explanation and justification of his position in karmic terms. The king thereby plays an important role as a kind of capstone to the social and political order. He serves as a reference point, defining the pinnacle of karma in human society and assuming a position of supremacy in social as well as political terms. All lines of patronage and all social hierarchies ultimately terminate with the king, at least in theory.[18] Even in modern Thai politics, the role of the king as a mediator between conflicting parties and politicians is preserved. Party leaders who wish to compromise without losing face in front of their followers by surrendering to rivals sometimes go through the ritual of having the king publicly dictate to them a compromise on which they may already have agreed. The compromise is thus ratified in the most credible way possible, and neither side has to concede the superiority of the other. They have been instructed by the king, who is superior to everyone.

---

[16] See Sharp and Hanks, *Bang Chan*, pp. 107-9. The authors discuss the case of a debt slave who became a *nakleng*, and eventually rose to become a village headman. It should be noted here that the possession of wealth is the best means to make merit, since "in general . . . it is accepted that the amount of beneficial karma that a person gains is directly related to the cost" of the merit-making activity involved. Terwiel, *Monks and Magic*, p. 218. For this reason, simply living a moral life according to the Buddha's Five Precepts is recognized as being meritorious, but is not ranked very high on lists of effective merit-making activities. Financing the building of a temple is usually considered the most meritorious activity. Terwiel, *Monks and Magic*, pp. 244-6, and Tambiah, *Buddhism and the Spirit Cults*, pp. 146-7. One of the most popular of the Jataka stories, about the previous lives of the Buddha, is that of his life as Prince Vessantara. The Prince gave away all his wealth, the lucky elephant that brought prosperity to his kingdom, and even his wife and children. While this may sound irresponsibly extravagant to Western ears, it generated such a tremendous amount of merit that the Prince was reborn in his next life as the Gautama Buddha. See Rhys Davids, trans., *The Questions of King Milinda*, vol. II (Delhi: Motital Banarsidass, 1975 [1890]), pp. 114-34. The act of giving in itself was regarded as the mark of great karmic achievement. This is because only one of great merit would have the resources and the inclination to give so generously. Superiors are thus even more effective at making merit than inferiors.

[17] Ishii, *Sangha, State and Society*, p. 15.

[18] For comparison, see Ruth Benedict's similar argument about the social role of the Japanese emperor. Ruth Benedict, *The Chrysanthemum and the Sword: Patterns of Japanese Culture* (New York: Houghton Mifflin, 1946), pp. 68-70.

Kings are sometimes popularly believed to have magical powers. Former kings may even become important supernatural protectors. King Chulalongkorn, for instance, has become the center of a widespread modern cult, in which people seek his assistance in winning the lottery, fending off bad luck, preserving themselves from danger, and so on. Stories are told of the magical powers he supposedly possessed and his continuing concern, after rebirth in heaven, for the Thai people.[19] His brother Prince Mahidol, who founded the first hospital in Thailand, has become an object of reverence for people with sick relatives and friends. His statue on the hospital grounds receives offerings daily. Akin notes that "such tales of supernatural power always center around great kings."[20] Even in death the meritorious can act as patrons with followers who bring them fame and power.

Although this superiority is a product of merit making, its use is not necessarily meritorious. Thai gangsters today, for instance, are often seen as having tremendous stores of merit because they are very successful, making lots of money and acquiring lots of followers. The sinfulness of their current actions only proves how much merit they must have accumulated in the past, since they are able to sin so successfully for so long. Government officials in the old system were also seen to have merit from past lives, because they had high birth in this life. They were capable of abusing that power, however, and often did.

Ordinarily, however, status and power were identified with good karma. As David Wyatt expresses it, Thais " . . . identified personal power with personal merit in the Buddhist sense and it gave to personal political and bureaucratic advancement an aura of religious attainment."[21] This meant that superiors held their position by virtue of superior merit, and the proof of this was their accumulation of wealth and power, which was linked schematically to having followers. Akin makes the causal logic very explicit:

> The evaluation of statuses was extremely important in Thai society. This evaluation was based mainly on the control of manpower, the amount of clients possessed by an individual. Status appears to have involved a religious element, the belief that a person attained higher status on account of his past religious merit, or Karma. One could look at the formal organization of the society as having a hierarchy of positions to be filled by persons who had just that much past merit for the specific positions.[22]

Karma justifies hierarchy, but it is important to note that Buddhism also supplies other standards for judging behavior. Status and power are not in themselves considered sufficient justification for whatever harm superiors may inflict on inferiors. There are independent conceptual resources for judging the behavior of superiors. This point is sometimes missed by those who claim that peasants are rendered quiescent by a belief in karma; while it is true that superiors are superior

---

[19] See นิธิ เอียวศรีวงศ์, *ลัทธิพิธีเสด็จพ่อ ร. ๕* [Nithi Aeusrivongse, *The Cult of Royal Father Rama V*] (Bangkok: Silapawatanatham, 2536).

[20] Akin Rabibhadana, *The Organization of Thai Society in the Early Bangkok Period, 1782-1873* (Ithaca: Cornell Southeast Asia Program, 1969), p. 53

[21] David Wyatt, "Family Politics in Nineteenth Century Thailand," *Journal of Southeast Asian History* 9,2 (1968): 211.

[22] Akin, *Organization of Thai Society*, p. 179.

due to their karma, it does not follow that everything they do is right. It only means that they are more effective at what they do. They can help more effectively, as well as punish more effectively and exploit more effectively. The karmic relationship binds superiors and inferiors in ties of self-interest; it does not impose blind obedience to authority. Buddhist peasants know when they are being abused.[23]

The concept of karma does not simply justify hierarchy. It also makes clientage a rational choice for the weak and patronage a demonstration of superiority for the strong. Merit is more than an ideological tool to legitimize power. It is also a concept that individuals, both powerful and weak, use to understand their relationships to the world and to other people. It provides one of the most fundamental schemata for social interaction and informs behavior in a way that makes hierarchical social relations seem normal, natural, and rational.

CLIENTAGE AND HIERARCHY

Clients not only indicate the status of their leader; in a more profound sense, they constitute it. In modern Thailand powerful monks have lots of lay followers; a monk with no followers cannot be very powerful. Powerful politicians have many supporters who supply votes or money; without votes and money politicians are powerless. Successful businessmen and bureaucrats from important government agencies are often lavishly generous; generosity brings them renown and increases the number of contacts who can be potentially utilized to advance their own endeavors. These activities not only cultivate the appearance of power, they also make people powerful.[24] The conceptual linkages between karma, power, and hierarchy are not just idealist constructions. They are confirmed by observing the world. In the pre-modern system followers were a source of prestige and dignity for the powerful, but these followers were also a source of wealth and a pool of labor.[25]

The political order that developed in this cultural and material environment thus emphasized the control of manpower as the primary constituent of power. This is not to say that other factors—money, land, title, and so on—were not important, but rather that controlling people was seen to be the single most important indicator and constituent of power. It was the primary way people conceived of power, and other resources were deployed to maximize it.

---

[23] See Katherine Ann Bowie, "Peasant Perspectives on the Political Economy of the Northern Thai Kingdom of Chiang Mai in the Nineteenth Century" (PhD Dissertation, University of Chicago, 1988), especially Chapter 2. It should be noted, however, that superiors are usually assumed to be wiser and better than inferiors until proven otherwise.

[24] For this reason merit is made publicly, earning both merit and prestige in the community. Ingersoll writes that this is "best understood as a *validation* of the very existence of merit by its becoming public knowledge. The gathering of one's reputation and karma are aspects of the same interpersonal-spiritual process." See Ingersoll, "Merit and Identity," p. 234.

[25] นันทิยา สว่างวุฒิธรรม, "การควบคุมกำลังคนในสมัยรัตนโกสินทร์ก่อนการจัดการเกณฑ์ทหาร (พศ ๒๓๒๕-๒๔๔๘)" [Nuntiya Swangvudthitham, "The Control of Manpower During the Bangkok Period Prior to the Introduction of Modern Conscription (BE 2325 – 2448)"] (MA Thesis in History, Chulalongkorn University, BE 2525), p. 183; and Lucien M. Hanks, "The Thai Social Order as Entourage and Circle," in *Change and Persistence in Thai Society*, pp. 197-218.

SAKDINA, TITLE, AND MANPOWER

The central government tried to control and display status and power in a number of ways. Its success depended in large part on how these attempts were received by provincial and local officials. Some attempts, such as the assignment of numerical ranks called *sakdina*, do not seem to have been very effective. Others, such as the assignment of titles and labor, meant a great deal more at the local level and were more effective.

H. G. Quaritch Wales translates *sakdina* as "dignity marks," although literally it means "power of the fields."[26] It may once have involved landholding in some way, but by the early Bangkok period the term had lost any connection with land and referred exclusively to a system of ranking people in the official hierarchy.[27] The king's *sakdina* was infinite, as he in theory controlled everyone and everything in the kingdom. The *sakdina* ranks of royalty ran from one hundred thousand down to five hundred, while those of officials ran from ten thousand down to four hundred. Ranks were a function of birth, conferred title, and appointed position. Those with *sakdina* of less than four hundred *rai* were all theoretically commoners, meaning they were subject to various forms of taxation, although as we shall see this issue was in practice much more complicated. Ordinary commoners—*phrai*—had *sakdina* of ten to twenty-five *rai*, and at the bottom of the scale came slaves and beggars, with *sakdina* of five *rai*. In theory everyone in the kingdom was ranked in a single hierarchy capped by the king.

Sakdina was significant only for officials in the capital, however. It is rarely mentioned in correspondence between the provinces and the capital; instead, this correspondence tends to involve titles and manpower. These were the things that were important to local officials, with manpower being by far the more important of the two.[28]

Title was important in the provinces, primarily because along with certain titles came the right to certain units of manpower. For instance, a *cao meuang*, the ruler of a town, had the right to command *phrai* known as *khong meuang*.[29] This meant that

---

[26] Quaritch Wales argues that this indicates a distant connection to a defunct system of control of land. This is supported by the fact that *sakdina* was measured in *rai*, a measure of land equivalent to approximately .4 acres. This situation was followed by an intermediate stage in which *sakdina* indicated the number of one's followers, so that, e.g., a *sakdina* of ten thousand *rai* indicated control of four hundred *phrai* with *sakdina* of twenty-five *rai* each. However, it is quite clear that for the entire historical record *sakdina* has been divorced from the actual control of land and has merely been a way of ranking the relative status of people. H. G. Quaritch Wales, *Ancient Siamese Government and Administration* (New York: Paragon Books, 1965 [1934]), pp. 49-50.

[27] Those who did not cultivate, such as beggars or palace craftsmen, still had *sakdina*. See also Sharp and Hanks, *Bang Chan*, p. 76.

[28] Wilson argues, however, that *sakdina* was more important prior to the Fourth Reign and then declined in significance. Constance Wilson, "State and Society in the Reign of King Mongkut, 1851-1868: Thailand on the eve of Modernization" (PhD Dissertation, Cornell University, 1970), p. 475.

[29] In Thai, คงเมือง. These were royal *phrai* in the provinces, usually *phrai suai*. In practice, however, these distinctions were often only theoretical, and in practice *nai* used all the *phrai* under their command as suited them, without respecting functional divisions. นันทิยา, "การควบคุมกำลังคน" [Nuntiya, "Control of Manpower"], pp. 28, 32, 158; อัญชลี สุสายัณห์, "ความเปลี่ยนแปลงของระบบไพร่และผลกระทบต่อสังคมไทยในรัชสมัยพระบาทสมเด็จพระจุลจอมเกล้า

being a *cao meuang* increased one's power by increasing the number of *phrai* under one's command. The prestige and power of the title in the end was caught up in the control over manpower it conferred.

Titles and *sakdina* were creations of the court by which it attempted to create avenues to power and prestige that it controlled exclusively. Clientage and hierarchy were enduring features of Thai social relations, however. They were not products of government policy; instead, government policy was adapted to use the social impulse towards hierarchy. This was an imperfect arrangement from the perspective of the court because people developed unofficial relationships. The fact remained that patronage continued to provide the primary way to power, and success was defined by the acquisition of many followers.

LAND AND MONEY

The dominance of clientage as a source and indicator of power was reinforced by the subordination of other potential sources of power. Land was not a source of power because it was abundant and because anyone could hold it. Without scarcity value, it had only the value given it by the labor that went into clearing it. Without attendant political value, it was not a source of power.

Money was not an important source of power either. There were no capitalists in old Siam who insisted on carefully defining their property rights.[30] Cash did circulate in the kingdom,[31] but the king had mechanisms to control who had it, and he could prevent large concentrations from accruing to people who were, from his perspective, undesirable. In the absence of indigenous industry, the wealthiest people in the country were court nobles and Chinese merchants. The former accumulated their wealth through the control of manpower or through special privileges granted by the king. By reassigning manpower, moving nobles to new, less lucrative positions, redefining their responsibilities, or revoking their privileges the king could seriously reduce their income.[32] In addition, most officials and nobles who

---

เจ้าอยู่หัว " [Anchalee Susayanha, "Changes of the Phrai System and Their Effects on Thai Society in the Reign of King Chulalongkorn"] (MA Thesis in History, Chulalongkorn University, BE 2524), p. 120. See Appendix I for a discussion of the various kinds of *phrai*.

[30] That is, people who accumulated and reinvested wealth for its own sake. I am employing Weber's distinction between greed and capitalism, the latter being characterized by the continuous and systematic pursuit of profit, reinvested to accumulate still more wealth, and so on. See Max Weber, *The Protestant Ethic and the Spirit of Capitalism*, trans. Talcott Parsons (London: Unwin Allen, 1930), p. 17.

[31] Koizumi demonstrates for instance that even in the economically relatively backward Northeast, commutation of taxes in kind to cash began on local initiative as early as the 1830s. This indicates that some quantity of cash, probably linked to trade, was circulating in the area. See Koizumi, "Commutation of *Suai*."

[32] In view of the argument to be presented in Chapter Four, it should be noted that court nobles were particularly vulnerable to the reassignment of their followers. These court nobles either lived near the capital, where the king was particularly powerful and where other, competing nobles were likely to have their own connections among commoners, or else they resided far from the capital, so that the court nobles were dependent on their official position to induce the officers who controlled them directly to cooperate. For court nobles the best way to preserve their *phrai* resources was to improve their position at court. For the officials at the local level good information about their *phrai* and good relations with them were the best

controlled tax-paying commoners were chronically in arrears on their taxes, which meant that in effect the king could bankrupt them at any time by calling in their tax payments. Chinese merchants usually made their living either through participation in the junk trade with China, which was dominated by royalty, or through tax farms granted by the king.[33] Both depended on the king's pleasure. The king thus controlled the main sources of revenue and could prevent the accumulation of cash from producing competing centers of power.

Social and political ideas mediated the relationships people had to these different potential sources of power. The Siamese could have controlled land more tightly by mapping it out and assigning rights to it, as happened in similarly underpopulated areas of the Eastern European frontier of the late Middle Ages or the nineteenth-century American frontier. Siamese officials could have tried to negotiate special privileges from the crown to protect urban manufacturers, as happened in medieval European cities. They did not, however, because these endeavors seemed unimportant to them. They would have been wasting their energy, when the really important goal was controlling labor in the form of followers. In Siam the direct control of people was the primary basis of power, was its best indicator, and was the way people conceived of power.

The central government tried to make the official political hierarchy as congruent as possible with the actual distribution of manpower in the kingdom. However, there were also conceptual resources people could draw on to cheat. There was always an incentive for patrons to hide unofficial clients who could provide them with untaxed resources. Thus the official hierarchy never perfectly matched the real situation. Furthermore, the government did not have sufficient information or resources to make the official system conform to reality. This will be discussed in greater detail below; the essential point here is that although the control of manpower was vitally important to politics, there was considerable difference between the way the system worked in theory and in fact. There were schemata for violating the law and challenging the official system, which were at least as important in shaping people's behavior as the official political theory.

POLITICAL THEORY IN THE EARLY BANGKOK PERIOD COURT

Official political theory in the early Bangkok period court focused on the monarchy. It was produced and reproduced by the court, in the form of legal codes and Buddhist texts. It emphasized the king and painted an exaggerated picture of his importance. This material is easily available and relatively concise and has therefore come to form the basis of a number of influential accounts of Thai government.[34] It

---

means to preserve their own following, since the court was generally reluctant to gamble on reassigning *phrai* and taking the chance of losing them from the system altogether.

[33] Royally sponsored trade became less important in the Third and Fourth Reigns, and the use of tax farmers increased in the same period. On the evolution of these institutions in the early Bangkok period, see Hong Lysa, *Thailand in the Nineteenth Century: Evolution of Economy and Society* (Singapore: Institute of Southeast Asian Studies, 1984), Chapters 3 and 4.

[34] Quaritch Wales, for instance, relies very heavily on the Three Seals Law, discussed below, as does Akin in his influential *Organization of Thai Society*. In addition to the Three Seals Law, other sources for Thai political theory in this period include various Buddhist texts, such as the *Questions of King Milinda* and the "Agganna Suttanta." These texts are emphasized by Tambiah in *World Conqueror and World Renouncer*.

must be understood that these documents reflect royal ambitions more than actual practice. Their function was not to educate administrators or judges in the practice of their vocations, but to provide intellectual resources to justify the king's authority.

The king had supreme authority over the law:

The power of the king was supreme to preserve the law, to interpret the law, and to create new law. There was no Parliament free to act as a legislative counterbalance. There was no tradition of a strong and independent judiciary which might create a system of common law. There was no Magna Carta standing between the king and subjects as a symbol of the rights and liberties of individuals which could be enforced against the king. In short, the essence of law was the king himself. The law was a justification of kingship, and the king was the interpreter and creator of law.[35]

Part of the reason there were no legal limitations on the king's power in Siam analogous to limitations imposed by the Magna Carta in England was that the content of the law was relatively unimportant in daily life. Most disputes were settled by mediation, as is still the case in Thai law.[36] When legal decisions were required, they were made by local officials who had little or no training in the law, who may never have seen a law book, and who prepared for their position by watching a prior office-holder at work.[37] Thus the lack of legal controls which led European observers to see the Thai king as an oriental despot really reflected not so much his absolute power as the limited importance of written law in Siamese government.

In the official court tradition, it has become customary to divide Thai conceptions of the monarchy into three ideal types, often represented as three historical moments in a dialectical fashion. The first, patriarchal kingship, is seen as opposed by the second, the Brahminical kingship of the *devaraja* (literally "god-king") cult. These two extremes are then moderated by the middle way, Buddhist kingship as expressed through the Thammasat.[38]

Sukhothai, conventionally identified as the first Thai kingdom, is said to have been characterized by patriarchal kingship. The king was a fatherly figure who cared

---

[35] David Engel, *Law and Kingship in Thailand during the Reign of King Chulalongkorn* (Ann Arbor: University of Michigan Center for South and Southeast Asian Studies, 1975), p. 8.

[36] William J. Klausner, *Reflections on Thai Culture: Collected Writings of William J. Klausner* (Bangkok: Siam Society, 1993), pp. 221-3, and David Engel, *Code and Custom in a Thai Provincial Court: the Interaction of Formal and Informal Systems of Justice* (Tucson: University of Arizona Press, 1978), p. 3.

[37] สมเด็จพระเจ้าบรมวงศ์เธอ กรมพระยาดำรงราชานุภาพ, *เทศาภิบาล* [Prince Damrong Rajanu-bhab, *Thesaphiban*] (Bangkok: Memorial Volume for *Phraya* Atkrawisunthon, BE 2503), p. 25. John Bowring comments on the difficulty of obtaining law books. See John Bowring, *Kingdom and People of Siam, Vol. I* (New York: Oxford University Press, 1969 [1857]), p. 174.

[38] This tradition stems from สมเด็จพระเจ้าบรมวงศ์เธอ กรมพระยาดำรงราชานุภาพ, *ลักษณะการปกครองประเทศสยามแต่โบราณ* [Prince Damrong Rajanubhab, *Characteristics of Ancient Siamese Government*] (Bangkok: Memorial Volume for Khun Sanitprachakon [Kulap Sukramun], BE 2524).

for his subjects as if they were his children and was always accessible to them. According to the King Ramkhamhaeng inscription, the king hung a gong by the palace gate that any commoner with a grievance could ring. The king would then emerge and dispense justice personally.[39]

After the center of Thai civilization moved south to Ayuthaya in the fourteenth century, it is said to have acquired a more absolutist character under the influence of Brahmins from the Khmer Empire. At this time the *devaraja* cult was introduced and the phrase "Lord of Life" came to be applied to the king. The close relationship between the king and his subjects disappeared, and the king became a distant and imposing figure; subjects were forbidden even to look at him.[40]

Buddhism is held to have moderated the extremity of the *devaraja* cult. While the Buddhist king's power remained, in theory, absolute, that absolutism was modified by the moral authority of the Dharma as expressed in the teachings of the Buddha and in the ancient Mon law code, the Thammasat. The Thammasat became the textual basis of Thai law in Ayuthaya and the early Bangkok period. The Buddhist king was supposed to deal compassionately with his subjects, as the patriarchal kings had done. Rama III thus set up a drum for petitioners to beat, symbolically recalling the gong of King Ramkhamhaeng and representing the ordinary person's privilege of seeking redress from the king.[41]

The source of law in this theory was the Thammasat. The role of the king was to rule in accordance with the law of the Thammasat and to protect the Buddhist religion. Technically the proclamations of kings did not themselves have the force of law; they derived their authority from the fact that the king, as the defender of the faith ruling in accordance with the Dharma, would only proclaim such laws as were appropriate to its preservation. The decrees of the king were simply emanations or instances of the eternal law. Royal adherence to the Dharma was associated with the universal monarch, or *chakravartin*.[42]

The role of kingship in this theory is illustrated by the myth told by the Gautama Buddha to his disciple Vasettha in the "Agganna Suttanta." Undifferentiated spirits, he says, once occupied an undifferentiated world. Then a pure food became available to them, which they ate for pleasure, although they did not need it for sustenance. These spirits gradually became more gross—physical, fleshy, disgusting, and less virtuous—as a consequence of consuming food. As their virtue declined, so did the quality of their food, which in turn made them more gross, less virtuous, and less self-sufficient, a pattern that intensified in a vicious cycle. Eventually the spirits

---

[39] The authenticity of this inscription, supposedly dating back to the thirteenth century, has recently come into question. See James R. Chamberlain, ed., *The Ram Khamhaeng Controversy: Collected Papers* (Bangkok: Siam Society, 1991). Regardless of the outcome of this debate, it is clear that the inscription was believed to be genuine in the Fifth Reign, and reflected what was considered an ancient tradition of Thai kingship. See Prince Dhani, "The Old Siamese Conception of the Monarchy," *Journal of the Siam Society* 36,2 (1947): 93-4.

[40] Akin, *Organization of Thai Society*, pp. 40-1; and Engel, *Law and Kingship*, p. 2.

[41] Walter Vella, *Siam Under Rama III, 1824-1851* (Locust Valley, N. Y.: J. J. Augustin, 1957), p. 16. Vella notes that despite the symbolism the actual ability of subjects to petition was limited.

[42] For a discussion of *chakravartin* generally see John Strong, *The Legend of King Ashoka: a Study and Translation of the Asokavadana* (Princeton: Princeton University Press, 1983); for the Siamese context specifically see Tambiah, *World Conqueror and World Renouncer*, Chapters 4, 5, and 6. The Siamese were familiar with the idea of the *chakravartin* through the *Traiphum*. For an English translation, see Frank E. and Mani B. Reynolds, trans., *The Three Worlds According to King Ruang: A Thai Buddhist Cosmology* (Berkeley: University of California Press, 1982).

reached a point where they were differentiated into male and female, some more attractive and more just than others, and all were forced to plant, harvest, and husk rice by their own labor. This led to private property, theft, lying, and violence. At this point, facing anarchy,

> . . . those beings went to the being among them who was the handsomest, the most capable, and said to him: Come now good being, be indignant at that whereat one should rightly be indignant, censure that which should rightly be censured, banish him who deserves to be banished. And we will contribute to thee a proportion of our rice.
>
> And he consented, and did so, and they gave him a proportion of their rice.
>
> Chosen by the whole people, Vasettha, is what is meant by Maha Samata, so Mahasamata (the Great Elect) was the first standing phrase to arise (for such a one). The Lord of the Fields is what is meant by Khattiya; so Khattiya (noble) was the next expression to arise. He charms by the Norm—by what ought (to charm)—is what is meant by Raja; so this was the third standing phrase to arise.[43]

This story brings out several features that are important to this theory of Buddhist kingship. One is that the king is a representative of the people. His job is to discipline them to live within Dharma, and they have symbolically chosen him to do this because they are incapable of doing it themselves; he is chosen because all spontaneously recognize that he is the best among them. His absolute authority is thus made consistent with his election—or, more accurately, his acclamation.[44]

As the protector of the Thammasat, the king is also the protector of the Buddhist religion. This is most clearly reflected in the king's continual interest in reforming the Sangha in order to maintain its effectiveness as a "field of merit," in which ordinary people can plant alms and reap good karma. Kings would periodically send monks abroad to be re-ordained in an ostensibly less corrupt foreign Sangha, and to collect uncorrupted scriptures. These monks would then purify the entire Siamese order. This was a crucial function of Buddhist kingship, without which it was thought that the Sangha would inevitably decline. If the Sangha is corrupt, then people cannot make merit effectively, and the king is therefore failing to protect Dharma.[45]

---

[43] T. W. and C. A. F. Rhys Davids, trans., *Dialogues of the Buddha*, part III (London: Pali Text Society, 1965), pp. 82-9.

[44] The belief that the king was traditionally elected is persistent among Thai elites. See for instance "King Prajadipok's Memorandum," document I. A., in *Siam's Political Future: Documents From the End of the Absolute Monarchy*, ed. Benjamin A. Batson (Ithaca: Cornell Southeast Asian Program Data Paper #96, 1974), p. 13. Prince Dhani reports that "no hard and fast rules exist as to how electors are qualified as such, but they were usually royal and temporal lords of the Realm sometimes doing their business in the presence, but not with the participation, of spiritual lords." See Prince Dhani, "The Old Siamese Conception of the Monarchy," p. 100. This seems to have been how Rama III, IV, and V were chosen, although it must be added that the only candidates seriously considered were from the royal family. The process could produce a king who was beholden to one or two very influential ministers. This was true of all three of these monarchs at the beginnings of their respective reigns. Partly for this reason, Chulalongkorn introduced the English rule of succession, which has been used ever since.

[45] The issue of Sangha reform is dealt with at length in Tambiah, *Buddhist Saints of the Forest* and *World Conqueror and World Renouncer*. On state—Sangha relations, see Ishii, *Sangha, State and Society*. By contrast, one of the reasons the British had such difficulty in governing Burma

The king's role as protector of the faith became an important basis for his authority in matters not directly implicated in the Dharma, such as warfare and tax collection. This is very clear in the Three Seals Law, for instance, which was a recension of the laws of Ayuthaya commissioned by King Rama I as part of his campaign to reconstruct the kingdom. The laws of Ayuthaya were themselves based on the ancient Mon Thammasat. In the Three Seals Law it is said that the king guards and promotes the Buddhist religion ". . . for the current and future benefit of his subjects, great and small," enabling them to make merit and thus improve their fate. For this reason, doing corvée or military service for the king is itself said to be meritorious.[46]

This political theory is meant to link the interests of the king and his subjects through the Buddhist religion. Buddhism supports and validates the king's role as its patron and protector. In his role as the sustainer of the faith, the king benefits not only the Sangha, but ordinary people as well, because through his efforts they are given the opportunity to make merit and thereby aspire to a better life now or in the future. The common people are thus obligated to obey and assist the king. He needs their resources to preserve the religion, so they can continue to make merit. Paying taxes and serving corvée thus became linked to religious goals and are meritorious in themselves.

This theme is repeated in later proclamations and in later reigns. A Second Reign law on the registration of *phrai* links this act to the recruitment of soldiers and the manufacture of arms. These were to be used to defend the kingdom against "the enemy's servants of war, so they will be unable to destroy the holy religion as its teachings have come down to us" — the enemy in this case being Burma.[47] Other kings emphasized their connection to the Buddhist religion in other ways. Rama III engaged in extensive temple building. Rama IV's activities as a reformist monk helped establish his credentials for the throne and demonstrated his kingly merit.[48]

Some effort appears to have been made to expose commoners to these ideas about kingship. Prince Dhani writes:

> This old conception of the monarchy, more especially the ethics of it, such as the tenfold kingly virtues, the quartet of proper conduct for the ideal monarch, and the theory of the wheel-turning universal sovereign, in Siamese *chakrapat*, are ever kept before the public eye in literature, in sermons and in any other channel of publicity.[49]

On the other hand, it is important to recognize that these texts were products of the court. They did not necessarily reflect local realities very accurately, and

---

was precisely that they refused to patronize the Sangha because of their commitment to non-interference in religious matters.

[46] *กฎหมายตราสามดวง จศ ๑๑๖๖* [Three Seals Law of CS 1166] vol. 5, พระราชกำหนดใหม่ #14, pp. 247-8.

[47] เสถียร ลายลักษณ์ และคนอื่นๆ รวบรวม, *ประชุมกฎหมายประจำศก* [Sathian Lailak et al., eds., Collected Laws], vol. 2 (Bangkok: Daily Mail Printing House, BE 2478), p. 2.

[48] Craig J. Reynolds, "The Buddhist Monkhood in Nineteenth-Century Thailand" (PhD Dissertation, Cornell University, 1972), pp. 69, 89.

[49] Prince Dhani, "The Old Siamese Conception of the Monarchy," p. 103.

provincial elites were not especially interested in disseminating them. While the status-oriented behaviors and habits justified by the concept of karma were reflected in daily life, the fully elaborated court tradition of the king as the *chakravartin* who elicited the spontaneous submission of the whole world was not. The texts that formed the basis of the court's political theory were only one select strand of Buddhism in Siam, and prior to the reforms of King Chulalongkorn it was not an especially influential strand.

At most these texts helped reinforce the authority of the king, as distinct from the power of the king. Authority refers to the right to take an action. In most cases royal rights to control activities at the local level, to tax, to draft corvée laborers, to make appointments of local officials, and so on, were unchallenged. Having the legal or moral authority to take an action did not necessarily mean it was prudent for the king to do so. His actual power over these matters was circumscribed by prudence. In practice it may have been wiser for the king to allow local and provincial officials a great deal of autonomy.

The ideas expressed in the political theory of the court were not especially influential in daily practice and might be dismissed as mystifications or false consciousness.[50] However, they were not entirely removed from reality. The monks and scholars of the court wanted the texts they wrote to make sense to people and to have popular appeal. In part they tried to tap into people's emotional attachment to Buddhism, but there was more to it: they also appealed to people's self-interest. It was in the interest of commoners to be able to improve their lives by making merit, and to be defended from their neighbor's evil deeds by the king's justice. It was a good thing for them to live under a king who would protect their property and their religion, and who would enable them to make merit effectively. Therefore, in theory, they should voluntarily provide the king with the resources he required in order to continue to supply them with these services and opportunities, by paying their taxes, registering and serving corvée, and so on.

In reality, of course, the last step did not necessarily follow. The goods supplied by the king were common goods. This meant that life under a good king presented what economists would call a free-rider problem: one gets the benefits of peace, prosperity, and religion from the king without paying for them, assuming that everyone else does pay. Since everyone's incentives are identical, the result could be mass defection, with no collective goods at all being provided because no one will pay for them. Each person hopes that his neighbors will cover the cost.[51] While the king had unlimited authority and sought unlimited power, it was clear he did not have unlimited information, and this created the possibility that many of his subjects would cheat on taxes and corvée. Thus, we need to examine how the system worked in practice in order to understand when, why, and how people obeyed.

---

[50] As in Cit Phumisak, "The Real Face of Thai Feudalism Today," available in translation as Chapter 2 in Craig Reynolds, *Thai Radical Discourse: The Real Face of Thai Feudalism Today* (Ithaca: Cornell Southeast Asia Program, 1987), esp. pp. 60-1, or ปิยะฉัตร, *ระบบไพร่* [Piyachat, *Phrai System*], p. 41.

[51] On collective goods, see Mancur Olson, *The Logic of Collective Action: Public Goods and the Theory of Groups* (Cambridge, MA: Harvard University Press, 1965).

Chapter 3

POLITICAL INSTITUTIONS AT THE GRASSROOTS

Most accounts of the political structure of the pre-modern Siamese kingdom adopt the perspective of the central government and follow a tradition begun by King Chulalongkorn in his "Royal Explanation," which describes the political system as it existed then and explains why it needed to be reformed.[1] According to this tradition the old political system was hopelessly inefficient because the king's will could not be enforced at the local level. In the peaceful old days this was acceptable, but in the modern age with predatory colonial powers surrounding Siam it created a dangerous situation which needed to be remedied.

Clearly there are some problems with this account. For one, the old days were hardly so peaceful: the Burmese had annihilated the kingdom of Ayuthaya, and the first three kings of the Bangkok period were engaged in almost continual warfare. Furthermore, it had always been true that kings wanted more control at the local level; if reform was such a straightforward process, why had no earlier king successfully implemented it? Previous kings had engaged in various reform measures designed to centralize power. These had little or no effect at the systemic level; they tended to be local and their effects temporary.[2]

---

[1] "พระราชดำรัสในพระบาทสมเด็จพระจุลจอมเกล้าเจ้าอยู่หัวทรงแถลงพระราชาธิบายแก้ไขการปกครอง แผ่นดิน" ["Proclamation of King Chulalongkorn Explaining the Improvements in the Administration of the Kingdom"] in ชัยอนันต์ สมุทวณิช และ ขัตติยา กรรณสูต รวบรวม, *เอกสาร การเมืองการปกครองไทย (พศ ๒๔๑๗ - ๒๔๗๗)* [Chai-anan Samudavanija and Khatthiya Kansut, eds., *Thai Political and Administrative Documents (BE 2417 - 2477)*] (Bangkok: Social Science Association of Thailand, BE 2532), pp. 72-99.

[2] ปิยะฉัตร ปิตะวรรณ, *ระบบไพร่ในสังคมไทย พศ ๒๔๑๑ - ๒๔๕๓* [Piyachat Pitawan, *The Phrai System in Thai Society BE 2411 - 2453*] (Bangkok: Thammasat University Press, BE 2526), pp. 99, 116-9, 122-3. จดหมายเหตุ ร. ๔ ๑๒๒๐/๕๕ provides a Fourth reign example of a reform of local administration which was ordered by the king but had no visible effect at the local level.

This is not to say that no change took place during the early Bangkok period, but only that kings were not very successful at implementing systemic changes that would have enhanced their power. The changes which did take place in the economy and in social life were by and large not under their control, and did not tend to their advantage. For further discussion of change from the Third to Fifth Reigns, see Chapter Five below.

The significance of the "Royal Explanation" has been widely misunderstood. This document was not an historical treatise: it was a manifesto for change. Chulalongkorn's goal in his account of the old system was to justify its destruction and replacement with a more centralized system. It is hardly surprising that he emphasized its shortcomings in terms of the goals he wanted to achieve with reform. As Hong Lysa has observed, " . . . the traditional economic and political system, if seen solely from the point of view of the King who was to destroy it, would be deprived of the context which gave it a raison d'être in the first place."[3]

Understanding how the old system was rational—how it made sense to those who worked within it—requires us to start from the bottom with the foundational grassroots relationships and to work our way up through the level of the province to the capital and finally to the king, rather than following the more usual route of starting with the king and the law codes, and assessing behavior at the local level against them. We will see that kings had always had the authority to change the political institutions of the kingdom, and that they had considerable power to do so, but that the logic of self-interest in the context of Siam's traditional political culture led kings to accept decentralization as a second-best strategy. It was the best outcome they could achieve under the circumstances, given the constraints and conflicts they faced.

NAI AND *PHRAI*

The foundation of the old Siamese political system was the relationship between *nai* and *phrai*. Superficially this relationship resembled that between a medieval lord and his serfs.[4] However, the variety of translations used for the term *phrai* is itself sufficient proof that it does not fit precisely any Western concept. Consider the contrast between, for instance, H. G. Quaritch Wales's "freemen," Nigel Brailey's "free peasants," James A. Ramsay's "peasants," and Akin's "commoners." Khachorn Sukhabhanij introduces the term "serfs," only to later reject it.[5] In reality *phrai* were

---

[3] Hong Lysa, *Thailand in the Nineteenth Century: Evolution of Economy and Society* (Singapore: Institute of Southeast Asian Studies, 1984), p. 5.

[4] This superficial resemblance has been the cornerstone of most Marxist accounts of Thai "feudalism," most importantly Cit Phumisak's "The Real Face of Thai Feudalism," available in translation as Chapter 2 of Craig Reynolds, *Thai Radical Discourse: The Real Face of Thai Feudalism Today* (Ithaca: Cornell Southeast Asia Program, 1987). It is not exclusively a Marxist position: Sharon Kay Mitchell Calavan even claims that Siamese "feudalism" was based on a system of estates. See her "Aristocrats and Commoners in Rural Northern Thailand" (PhD Dissertation, University of Illinois at Champagne-Urbana, 1974), p. 6.

[5] H. G. Quaritch Wales, *Ancient Siamese Government and Administration* (New York: Paragon Books, 1965 [1934]), p. 43; Nigel Brailey, "The Origins of the Siamese Forward Movement in Western Laos: 1850-92" (PhD Dissertation, University of London, 1968), p. 27; James Ansil Ramsay, "The Development of a Bureaucratic Polity: The Case of Northern Siam" (PhD Dissertation, Cornell University, 1971), pp. 11, 43; Akin Rabibhadana, *The Organization of Thai Society in the Early Bangkok Period, 1782-1873* (Ithaca: Cornell Southeast Asia Program, 1969); and ขจร สุขพานิช, *ฐานันดรไพร่* [Khachorn Sukhabhanij, *The Status of Phrai*] (Bangkok: History Department, Si Nakharinwirot University at Prasanmit, BE 2519), p. 1. The term "commoners" is probably the safest and least misleading simply because it is the least specific, although

defined by their relationship to their *nai*, and this relationship was quite different from that of European lords and serfs.

Nai is easier to translate than *phrai* only because it is less specific. Generically it means a master or superior.[6] The more specific term *munnai* was used to refer to someone who directly controlled *phrai* officially registered to him.[7] The real meaning of both *nai* and *phrai* is to be found not in any precise English translation, but in the relationship which mutually defined them.[8]

The *nai-phrai* relationship cannot be adequately understood by an analogy to European medieval lords and serfs because those people were bound to each other by a piece of land which involved them in specific contractual obligations that were alien to the old Siamese political system. The relationship between *nai* and *phrai* was neither contractual nor based on land. It was instead overwhelmingly personalistic and was rooted in Thai schemata concerning inequality, patronage, and merit.

Phrai were followers and *nai* were leaders and patrons. *Phrai* might be of many different types: *luang* (royal) or *som* (private); captive or volunteer; *suai* (taxed in kind) or corvée; soldiers or civilian; Thai, Mon, Malay, Khmer, or Lao. In some cases slaves were referred to as *phrai*, in other cases low level *nai* were.[9] Most of these distinctions were in fact academic. The vast majority of *phrai* of all kinds were farmers who were used indiscriminately by their *nai* for a variety of tasks.[10]

The *nai* would choose who performed which tasks; it was a good idea for the *phrai* to try to cultivate good relations with him. A *nai* might, for instance, have his *phrai* cultivate fields for him. They would also ordinarily give him "gifts" of rice, fruit, vegetables, or whatever else they happened to produce. When tax time rolled

---

strictly speaking it is inaccurate because there is another term in Thai which means specifically commoner (*khon saman*).

The terms "serf" and "freeman" both connote specific legal conditions, both of which are misleading in the Thai context. "Peasant" is a loaded term theoretically, carrying with it a class analysis which would be misleading. In fact, it would be technically inaccurate, since the people in question in effect owned the means of production—but to call *phrai* capitalists would also be incorrect and would ridiculously distort their actual status.

[6] Akin, *Organization of Thai Society*, p. 79.

[7] On the term *munnai*, see ขจร, ฐานันดรไพร่ (Khachorn, *Status of Phrai*), pp. 9-13; and Constance Wilson, "State and Society in the Reign of King Mongkut, 1851-1868: Thailand on the eve of Modernization" (PhD Dissertation, Cornell University, 1970), pp. 586-8. The vast majority of *nai* were men, so I will use the masculine pronoun to refer to them. There are, however, rare cases of female *nai*, for instance noble women who were allowed to retain the *phrai* of their husbands after being widowed, (e.g. ร. ๕ บ ๑๗/๓๘), or female members of the royal family who were granted followers. See Wilson, "State and Society," p. 329.

[8] As is true of any relationship between a master and servant, a point famously made by Hegel in *Phenomenology of Spirit*. See G. W. F. Hegel, *Phenomenology of Spirit*, trans. A. V. Miller (New York: Oxford University Press, 1977), pp. 111-9.

[9] On slaves see for instance ร. ๔ รล-กห ๑๖/๕๖, ร. ๕ บ ๑๗/๔๕, or บ ๑๗/๕๒; on *nai* see ร. ๕ บ ๑๗/๘.

[10] See Appendix I for a discussion of the various types of *nai* and *phrai*.

around the *nai* might detail some *phrai* to pan for gold, pick cardamom, make bricks, or do corvée, depending on the particular obligations expected of them. If there were a war or a royal procession he would decide which *phrai* performed the duties for the group, usually getting the year's regular taxes remitted in the process.

At the lowest level of administration were officials called a *nai muat* or *nai kaung,* literally "*nai* of a group."[11] Although *nai* is usually translated as lord, master, or noble, at this level the term "foreman" might be more appropriate. Not all *nai muat* even had the minimum *sakdina* of four hundred, which would qualify them legally as officials. In the Fifth Reign they generally seem to have had titles such as *phra, luang,* or *khun,* all of which can have *sakdina* of more or less than four hundred.[12]

The social position of the *nai muat* seems to have varied geographically. In the Northeast, for instance, they were often among the most powerful local officials. In some Northeastern towns, the population was divided into four large *muat,* with each of the four major officials of the town having control of one.[13] In other places *nai muat* had a status only barely above that of the *phrai* themselves.[14] In some cases commoners seem to have become *nai muat* simply by gathering a following of unmarked *phrai* and volunteering to bring them into the official hierarchy.[15]

The *nai* was defined primarily by his function, which was to keep track of his *phrai* and make their labor and resources accessible to the higher levels of government. In exchange he was able to use his *phrai* for his own purposes as well.

---

[11] These terms seem to have been used interchangeably. Sometimes there were officers under *nai muat* called *palat muat,* or deputies. These were probably usual only in exceptionally large *muat* or *kaung,* or in cases where high officials wanted to be *nai muat* in order to control directly a group of *phrai,* but did not want to be bothered with the day-to-day administration of the group.

[12] See, e.g., ร. ๕ ม ๒๘.๒/๒๔ or "ทำเนียบข้าราชการนครศรีธรรมราชครั้งรัชกาลที่ ๒" ("List of Officials of Nakhon Si Thammarat in the Second Reign"] in *ประชุมพงศาวดาร* [*Collected Chronicles*] vols. 45 and 46 (Bangkok: Department of Fine Arts, BE 2518). On *nai kaung* generally, see Constance Wilson, "The *Nai Kong* in Thai Administration, 1824-68," *Contributions to Asian Studies* 15 (1980), pp. 41-57.

[13] บุญรอด แก้วกันหา, "การเก็บส่วยในสมัยรัตนโกสินทร์ตอนต้น (พศ ๒๓๒๕ - ๒๔๑๑)" [Boonrod Keawkanha, "The Collection of Suay During the Early Ratanakosin Period (AD 1782 - 1868)"] (MA Thesis in History, Chulalongkorn University, BE 2518), p. 72.

[14] อัญชลี สุสายัณห์, "ความเปลี่ยนแปลงของระบบไพร่และผลกระทบต่อสังคมไทยในรัชสมัยพระบาท สมเด็จพระจุลจอมเกล้าเจ้าอยู่หัว" [Anchalee Susayanha, "Changes of the Phrai System and their Effects on Thai Society in the Reign of King Chulalongkorn"] (MA Thesis in History, Chulalongkorn University, BE 2524), p. 62; and ธีรชัย บุญมาธรรม, "ประวัติศาสตร์ท้องถิ่นของ หัวเมือง กาฬสินธุ์, พศ ๒๓๓๖-๒๔๕๐" [Theerachai Boonmathum, "A Local History of Hua-muang Kalasin, 1793 – 1907"] (MA Thesis in History, Chulalongkorn University, BE 2528), p. 45.

[15] This at least is the claim of *Caophraya* Mahinthaun in a letter to King Chulalongkorn, ร. ๕ รล-พศ ๓/๑๓๑, pp. 142-3.

He received gifts from his *phrai* and a cut of their taxes, as well as the honor and dignity of having followers and official recognition.[16]

Although *nai* were appointed from above, these appointments had to recognize the preferences of those with local power, which might include bandits, *nakleng*, or popular monks. Johnston describes such appointments as alliances between the appointer and the appointed " . . . in which the latter agreed to see that his unit conformed generally to the needs of the whole in exchange for assurances that the whole would impinge no more than necessary on his unit."[17]

The *nai's* jurisdiction was purely personal. It was not geographical, because he could have *phrai* scattered across several villages or even provinces.[18] It was also not bureaucratic, because the duties of the *nai* were general, covering law, taxation, corvée, welfare, and anything else that the government might want from the *phrai* or the *phrai* might want from their patron. Only very general official rules governed his behavior towards those under his charge, and the character of the relationship varied a great deal from *nai* to *nai*. What defined the *nai* was the fact that he had charge of a group of *phrai*.

A *nai* was personally responsible for his *phrai*, for their taxes, corvée duties, and for producing them in court in case of legal trouble. Above all else, these functions required that he know his *phrai* personally, be able to recognize and find them, and be a good patron to them. This was the most crucial job in the old system. The *nai* provided the link between his *phrai* and the government. The *phrai's* allegiance to him represented their allegiance to the system.

Phrai were usually acquired through inheritance or by attaining official position, certain offices having royal *phrai* attached to them. They could also be gathered by "convincing" unmarked *phrai* to come into the system.[19] "Convincing" here should be understood very broadly; it was sometimes a euphemism for highly coercive behavior. Rama IV, for instance, instructed officials of Luang Prabang to attack the city of Chiang Rung with the aim of "convincing" the ruler of the city, his family, and their followers to resettle within Luang Prabang.[20] This practice seems to have been exceptional, though. Given the ease and frequency with which *phrai* could flee, and the poor communications and transportation available, sheer force alone could not

---

[16] นันทิยา สว่างวุฒิธรรม, "การควบคุมกำลังคนในสมัยรัตนโกสินทร์ก่อนการจัดการเกณฑ์ทหาร (พศ ๒๓๒๕ - ๒๔๔๘)" [Nuntiya Swangvudthitham, "The Control of Manpower During the Bangkok Period Prior to the Introduction of Modern Conscription (BE 2325-2448)"] (MA Thesis in History, Chulalongkorn University, BE 2525), p. 183.

[17] David Bruce Johnston, "Rural Society and the Rice Economy in Thailand, 1880-1930" (PhD Dissertation, Yale University, 1975), pp. 158-9.

[18] ร. ๕ บ ๑๗/๘, ๑๗/๖๙, and "ประกาศเปลี่ยนการควบคุมเลก" ["Decree Changing the Control of *Phrai*"] in เสถียร ลายลักษณ์ และคนอื่นๆ รวบรวม, *ประชุมกฎหมาย ประจำศก* [Sathian Lailak et al., eds., *Collected Laws*] vol. 17 (Bangkok: Daily Mail Printing House, BE 2478), p. 69.

[19] The Thai term is *kliaklaum* (เกลี้ยกล่อม), meaning to convince or induce.

[20] จดหมายเหตุ ร. ๔ ๑๒๑๔/๑๖. *Phrai* of Sipsaung Panna were also included in this mandate. The letter further notes that the deputy ruler of Chiang Rung and six thousand followers had been "convinced" to settle in Nan by an earlier raid. Both Luang Prabang and Nan were tributaries of Bangkok at this time.

have maintained this system. Force could be mobilized for relatively short periods for specific objectives, but a police state based on constant mobilization and surveillance would not have been possible. *Phrai* therefore had to be accommodated and induced to stay.

Indeed, Rama IV also declined a request to allow the rulers of the southern Lao town of Attopeu to raise troops in order to put down a rebellion by *phrai* who had murdered an official sent to collect their *suai* (taxes in kind). The king suspected that they had been oppressed by the local officials, but more importantly " . . . if they can come together as a group they may fight, and if they cannot fight they may flee to the forest. . . . I am worried that then other *phrai* who pay *suai* and *phrai* of nearby towns will become alarmed and flee to the forest."[21] Keeping *phrai* in the system thus could even take precedence over preserving order and supporting local officials.

Phrai were inherited, on the assumption that an heir was more likely to be familiar with the *phrai* than anyone else.[22] Occasionally a *nai* would die without leaving behind anyone personally familiar with his *phrai*. This could entail the loss of the whole group to the system, a disaster for the intermediate officials to whom the *nai* had been responsible, but who would still be held accountable for those *phrai*. This produced draconian results in some places. There are reports of some towns jailing *phrai* for indefinite periods after the death of their *nai*, for no other reason than that the town officials were afraid they would be lost or flee before they could be assigned to another *nai*. The more common case was that a *nai* would train his prospective heir by familiarizing him with his future clients.[23]

The death, crippling, or flight of *phrai* was a perennial problem for *nai*. Since they were in theory responsible for the taxes of all the *phrai* registered to them, the loss of *phrai* inevitably led to overassessments and underpayment. In the Fifth Reign it might require a petition to the throne to have these arrears forgiven, itself an expensive and complex process.[24] This meant an even heavier burden on the *phrai* who remained, which would in turn encourage them to flee or to find another patron.

The logical solution for the *nai* was to underreport the number of *phrai* under his control. This had two beneficial results for the *nai*: it provided a cushion, so that some loss of *phrai* could be tolerated, and it produced some extra income because the *nai* could use the labor and produce of the unregistered *phrai* himself. Another strategy was simply to underpay taxes. Virtually every *nai* as well as every village and town in the kingdom was chronically in arrears.[25] These strategies benefited the *phrai* as

---

[21] จดหมายเหตุ ร. ๔ ๑๒๑๘/๑๓๘ (draft) and ๔๘ (clean copy).

[22] "ประกาศเรื่องชำระเลขเจ้าสิ้นพระชนม์นายถึงแก่กรรม" ["Proclamation on the Disposition of the *Phrai* of Deceased *Cao* and Dead *Nai*"], in เสถียร, *ประชุมกฎหมายประจำสก* [Sathian, *Collected Laws*] vol. 11, pp. 117-9, and นันทิยา, "การควบคุมกำลังคน" [Nuntiya, "Control of Manpower"], p. 128.

[23] ร. ๔ รล-กห ๑/๔๗; ปิยะฉัตร, *ระบบไพร่* [Piyachat, *Phrai System*], p. 103.

[24] Virtually the entire correspondence of *Krom* Phrasurasawadi in the Fifth Reign is filled up with these requests. They are common in other files as well.

[25] Some tax assessments had unbelievably poor returns. Anchalee reports one which was 92.05% uncollected after two years. See อัญชลี, "ระบบไพร่" [Anchalee, "Phrai System"], p. 260-1. The central government regularly offered discounts on tax arrears paid within a stipulated

well as the *nai*, since the overall tax burden was reduced and the benefits could be distributed as patronage. Thus, *nai* and *phrai* had an incentive to conspire to defraud the government in matters such as registration and taxes. Such behavior violated the law, but it was common and tolerated, in much the same way that speeding is in the US. In both cases, illegal behavior which is difficult to police becomes an accepted part of the political culture. Excessively strenuous attempts to enforce the law may actually violate people's sense of propriety.

Phrai wanted good crops, low taxes, peace, and the opportunity to make merit effectively, with no corvée, no legal troubles, and no bandits. In effect this meant that they wanted to have as little direct contact with the government as possible, while enjoying the order, legal benefits, and religious opportunities it could provide.

These goals could not all be maximized simultaneously. Suppressing bandits might require a royal commissioner to come out from the capital to draft *phrai* to hunt the criminals down, and this would also mean corvée and tax collections. Avoiding legal trouble required registering under a *nai* and paying at least some taxes. Furthermore, the king was recognized as having a legitimate claim on local resources for things like maintaining the Sangha as an effective field of merit and defending the kingdom. Balancing these goals meant engaging in complex negotiations with *nai* and central government officials, and weighing the costs and benefits of a variety of strategies.

PHRAI STRATEGIES

A variety of strategies were available to *phrai* for achieving a favorable mix of outcomes given their particular situation, ranging from the least to the most cooperative. The most extreme non-cooperative strategy was flight: to abandon all patronage. Since they were not bound to any specific piece of land, *phrai* could and did move. The benign environment made it relatively easy to find food and clear new fields, so they could move to unpopulated sections of wilderness where they would be free of their *nai* and government generally.[26] The forests of Siam were sufficiently dense and the mountains sufficiently rugged that it would be virtually impossible to find people who did not want to be found. Further, there were almost no roads, only paths through the jungle easily and often obscured by treefalls. Maps were rare and inaccurate. Most transportation was by water, but even near the waterways *phrai* seem to have been relatively safe. The village of Bang Chan, made famous by the Cornell Study Project in the 1950s, was founded by such fugitive *phrai* on a small

period of time in order to encourage at least partial payments. See ปิยะฉัตร, *ระบบไพร่* [Piyachat, *Phrai System*], pp. 116-27; สมเด็จพระเจ้าบรมวงศ์เธอ กรมพระยาดำรงราชานุภาพ, *เทศาภิบาล* [Prince Damrong Rajanubhab, *Thesaphiban*] (Bangkok: Memorial Volume for *Phraya* Atkrawisunthon, BE 2503), pp. 50-1; and เสถียร, *ประชุมกฎหมายประจำศก* [Sathian, *Collected Laws*] vol. 9, p. 239 and vol. 11, pp. 13-4.

[26] There are numerous cases in the National Archives of fugitive *phrai* being discovered by *nai*. See for instance ร. ๔ รล-กห ๑๑/๑๕, ร. ๕ บ ๑๗/๓๑, and รล-มท ๑๖/๑๑๙. Even more visible are the effects: there are innumerable requests in the files of *Krom* Phrasurasawadi in the Fifth Reign from *nai* asking to subtract from their rolls *phrai* who have fled or who are otherwise unavailable for taxation.

stream feeding the Rangsit canal. Despite its proximity to Bangkok the Bang Chan villagers reported that they had very little to do with the central government until the twentieth century, which seems to indicate that flight was a viable strategy even in the relatively densely populated area of the capital.[27] *Phrai* were supposed to be registered and tattooed at age eighteen, but it was not uncommon for officials to catch unregistered *phrai* who were thirty or forty years old.[28]

Flight was attractive to *phrai* who felt abused by their *nai*, overtaxed, or who thought they could improve their status by striking out on their own. It meant an end to taxes and corvée, and to whatever other exactions that *nai*, *nakleng*, or other villagers were demanding. However, flight also entailed serious disadvantages, as fugitives had to endure a lean year or two until the new fields could be cleared and brought into production, they were exposed to bandits and wild beasts, they completely lacked legal protection,[29] and they were hampered in their ability to make merit, since monks and temples were found in villages, not in the woods. There was also the risk that one's old *nai* would track one down, in which case all the resources invested in moving and starting a new farm would be wasted.

This strategy was probably easiest on the Central Plains. In the mountains and jungles of the North and South and the dry plateau of the Northeast, starting a new farm would have been a more daunting endeavor.

The difference between being a fugitive and being part of the kingdom lay in the act of registration. *Phrai* who entered the system formally did so by being registered to a *nai*. The *nai* would make up a list of their numbers, and often even their names, to send to the central government.[30] Registered *phrai* would be tattooed on the wrist or the back of the hand, depending on the reign, with their name, the name of their father, their place of residence, and the name of their *nai*.[31] They would then be liable for taxes and corvée. In return they could live in towns and villages with frequent

---

[27] Lauriston Sharp and Lucien M. Hanks, *Bang Chan: Social History of a Rural Community in Thailand* (Ithaca: Cornell University Press, 1978), pp. 64-5.

[28] นันทิยา, "การควบคุมกำลังคน" [Nuntiya, "Control of Manpower"], p. 160.

[29] As Hong Lysa points out, protection from the government was one of the main functions of *nai*. See Hong, *Thailand in the Nineteenth Century*, p. 27.

[30] These rolls were called *hangwaw*, "kite's tails," because of their length. *The Three Seals Law* actually stipulated that the *phrai* be listed individually by name, but in practice often only the numbers and types of *phrai* registered to a *nai* were recorded. See กฎหมายตราสามดวง พระราชกำหนดเก่า #14, vol. 5 (Bangkok: Department of Fine Arts, n.d.), pp. 1-6. Normally only adult males were recorded. The *hangwaw* were the basis of the government's tax and corvée demands. Occasionally a more elaborate census of family members, houses, and cattle was made, called *samano khrua*; this term later evolved into the Thai translation of the English word "census."

[31] Specialists were employed for this purpose by *Krom* Phrasurasawadi and by units called *Krom* Satsadi in the larger *meuang*, the organizations charged with maintaining the rolls. *Nai* in the smaller *meuang* either sent their *phrai* to the capital to be tattooed or waited for the sporadic tattooing units sent out from the capital. These latter would be headed by a major noble and would attempt to sweep the area. *Nai* would be instructed to bring in their *phrai* to be tattooed by a certain date, after which patrols would comb the area to catch any untattooed *phrai* and register them as royal *phrai*.

opportunities to make merit, and enjoy physical and legal protection from bandits, wild beasts, and malicious lawsuits.

The most extreme cooperative strategy was to sell oneself into bondage, becoming a *that*. The term *that* is usually translated as slave, but this was not chattel slavery.[32] Even those who became slaves as war captives had certain legal rights and were not simply property. Most slaves were really debt bondsmen or indentured servants. Men could sell their wives, children, or themselves into slavery; in exchange they received not only money but also security. Their master was now bound to feed them and take care of them, and they were taxed at a much lighter rate than *phrai*. Bondage did reduce their status, though, binding them permanently to the master's household as servants. This was the polar opposite of flight; rather than electing to flee an exacting *nai* and pursue an uncertain future unbound to political society, one threw oneself on the mercy of the master hoping he would treat his servants kindly. This extreme dependence on a superior was conceptually linked with extremely low status in the karmic hierarchy. But, although the slave's position was lowly, it was also the most secure possible in political society.

More often *phrai* decided to mediate between these extremes, remaining within the political system and trying to arrange the best deal they could. The potential for flight gave the *phrai* some leverage against the *nai*, which was amplified by the possibility of fleeing, not to the woods, but to another *nai*.

Phrai who felt they could get a better deal from another *nai* could and did switch masters, although this was technically illegal and hazardous for their new *nai*. There were strict laws against poaching the *phrai* of another *nai*, because any disturbance of the manpower registered in the *hangwaw* meant a decrease in the central government's control over the *phrai* themselves. In fact, however, *nai* often competed with each other for *phrai*.[33]

A good *nai*—one who could protect his *phrai* effectively—would attract more *phrai* from less effective *nai*. Easy mobility and the difficulty of tracking *phrai* except through their *nai* made this feasible. It was unlikely that the *phrai* would be caught by their old *nai*, and even if he did locate them, recovering them would require lengthy and expensive legal action against the new *nai*.[34] At the end of such a case the *phrai*

---

[32] On slavery, see Chatchai Panananon, "Siamese 'Slavery': The Institution and its Abolition" (PhD Dissertation, University of Michigan, 1982), esp. Chapter 2, on different varieties of slavery. See also Andrew Turton, "Thai Institutions of Slavery," in *Asian and African Systems of Slavery*, ed. James L. Watson (Berkeley: University of California Press, 1980), p. 262. Turton notes that Siam once had institutions resembling chattel slavery, with slavers trading in war captives and primitive tribespeople. However, " . . . from the early nineteenth century all slaves were progressively assimilated to a legal category of slaves by purchase," by which he means debt bondage. Such bondage was often the only way ordinary farmers could raise capital.

[33] Lorraine Gesick, "Kingship and Political Integration in Traditional Siam, 1767-1824" (PhD Dissertation, Cornell University, 1976), p. 175.

[34] This was true even if the *phrai* wanted to return. One *phrai*, named Suk, who was registered to a *munnai* inside the Grand Palace, spent seven months chained on the porch of the *Cao Meuang* of Nonthaburi, the province immediately north of Bangkok. It took this long for his *nai* to get a royal order to have Suk returned. The case was complicated by the fact that Suk had not been tattooed. The *Cao* of Nonthaburi had received an order to build several ships, which spurred him to dispatch agents to catch any unmarked *phrai* they could find in the area, presumably so that he would not have to draw on the labor of his own people. Suk and another *phrai* named Klaum had been caught with weapons after a rash of cattle thefts, but

were often simply asked which *nai* they preferred. Pursuit also entailed the risk that the recaptured *phrai* might claim that they had fled to escape unjust treatment under the old *nai*, and these complaints could cause the pursuer, and not the new *nai*, to be punished. Even if the *phrai* did return to their old *nai*, the new *nai* was seldom punished very severely. The whole process was thus decidedly chancy, and it is unsurprising that there are very few records of *nai* attempting to recover *phrai*.[35]

LAW AND POLICY

The law governing the relationship between *nai* and *phrai* was thus at odds with actual policy. Legally any change from the status quo registered in the rolls was punishable, but the policy was, in effect, to be lenient and allow *phrai* to choose the best deals they could get. Yet this could only mean the erosion of the accuracy of the rolls, collected at such a great cost in energy and resources.

In fact there was evasion and conspiracy at all points of the process and at all levels of the system. This is because it was in the interests of both *nai* and *phrai* to resist the demands of the capital and, paradoxically, it was actually in the interest of the king to tolerate this behavior, at least to a degree. Yet the system was not as self-subverting as it may seem.

The best way to conceive of the old system is as a complex series of negotiations. *Nai*, *phrai*, and king were all trying to advance their interests while having only limited information about each others' needs and resources.

The *nai* wanted as many people as possible under his control, since that made him more powerful. He wanted to extract as much labor and resources from his *phrai* as possible, but a good *nai* also understood that he would have to moderate his demands or else he would start to lose *phrai* to other *nai*. Such *nai* would be identified by *phrai* as more effective and powerful, and this would soon be demonstrated through the *nai*'s acquisition of more followers.

The *nai* depended on the higher levels of government too. He needed help to protect his followers if bandits became too numerous or bold, for instance. His recognition as an official by the central government also bolstered his status and implicit claim to karmic superiority. Maintaining this official position in the government required him to pass on some of the benefits he got from the *phrai*. He would have to pay some taxes, for instance, or be subject to legal action, but he would pay as little as he thought he could get away with, in part so that he could demand less from his *phrai*. The central government might also reward loyal and effective *nai* with more *phrai*; these might come from a master who died without an heir, from one being punished, or they might be *phrai* acquired through military campaigns.

The central government had to tolerate some defiance from both *nai* and *phrai*, because it had to balance its own aims, which could not all be maximized simultaneously. The government wanted high tax revenues, for instance, and detailed information about the numbers and location of *phrai* so that it could extract taxes effectively. On the other hand, it lacked the means to collect such information. The government lacked direct personal connections with *phrai* and was unable to

---

this criminal detail quickly dropped out of the discussion of the case, and Klaum, who was tattooed, was soon released. See ร. ๕ บ ๑๗/๕.

35 นันทิยา, "การควบคุมกำลังคน" [Nuntiya, "Control of Manpower"], pp. 151, 166.

judge local conditions very precisely, and such information is crucial for a government taxing peasants who live near subsistence levels. Being too effective at taxation could have the effect of driving *phrai* out of the system altogether, which would obviously be detrimental in the long run.[36] Only the *nai* who had constant and direct contact with their *phrai* knew how much they could reasonably be expected to pay.[37] *Nai* had an incentive to underreport, of course, so the central government periodically sent people out to tattoo and register *phrai*, in order to improve the capital's knowledge of the local situation, and the government would pursue at least some cases of tax arrears. They could never get completely accurate rolls, however, and they certainly could not have prosecuted everybody who owed back taxes,[38] so these exercises amounted to checking up on the *nai* and giving them some modest incentive to be honest and thorough. At the same time, by tolerating the movement of *phrai* and the underpayment of taxes, the capital was allowing *nai* to moderate their demands on the *phrai*, giving them the tools they needed to induce the *phrai* to stay within the system. It was actually in the interest of the central government to allow the *nai* and *phrai* to conspire against it—within limits. The capital always retained final sanction: it could dismiss *nai* and reassign *phrai* to someone else. Thus the competition between *nai* for *phrai* could also be made to serve the central government.

No system is entirely without opposition, and in old Siam local opposition did organize under alternative forms of leadership. These leaders were people who could tap into schemata for karmic authority, but who were not integrated into the official hierarchy. They threatened to draw people out of the official hierarchy or drive them out of the system altogether. The *nai* was not the only source of authority at the local level, and in the absence of sustained central government interest in their particular locale, *nai* often found it necessary to cooperate with these alternative leaders.

ALTERNATIVE SOURCES OF LOCAL ORDER AND DISORDER

Banditry

Banditry was endemic in rural Siam. Mostly it took the form of cattle rustling by competing gangs of youths: the *nakleng* mentioned above. Most villages had such gangs, and they would defend their own village and raid others. This made them

---

[36] John Murdoch argues that the effectiveness of colonial regimes at collecting regular, fixed taxes and enforcing rent payments provoked the 1901-2 "Holy Men's" Rebellions in the Mekong basin. See John B. Murdoch, "1901-2 'Holy Man's' Rebellion," *Journal of the Siam Society* 62,1 (1974): 47-66. James Scott presents a more general version of this argument. See James Scott, *Moral Economy of the Peasant: Rebellion and Resistance in Southeast Asia* (New Haven: Yale University Press, 1976), Chapter 3.

[37] For instance, Nuntiya reports on some *nai* who released their *phrai* from corvée duty so that they could go work in their fields. This is the sort of requisite knowledge of local agricultural conditions which central officials did not possess; if not released, these *phrai* would have been more inclined to try and escape a system that failed to accommodate their needs to feed themselves and their families. นันทิยา, "การควบคุมกำลังคน" [Nuntiya, "Control of Manpower"], p. 77.

[38] Not even the modern state with all its sophisticated information-gathering technology can do that. See Margaret Levi, *Of Rule and Revenue* (Berkeley: University of California Press, 1988). See especially Chapters 7 and 8.

heroes in one place and bandits in another. Under a particularly able leader or in times of dearth such gangs might develop into more dangerous criminal organizations.

Some bandits became very powerful, acquired central government officials as their patrons and developed extensive networks with other gangs. If they remained locally popular they could be very difficult to catch because the local people would protect them. They might also be shielded by the cooperation of local officials.[39] Often they would develop a reputation for supernatural powers which would further induce villagers to help them, out of fear and respect for a karmic superior.[40] Such figures thus might find themselves in an excellent position to integrate themselves into the government hierarchy through their wealth, local power, and claim to karmic authority.

Bandits represented both order and disorder at the local level. Their activities could cause trouble for two reasons. First, their depredations might terrorize an area to such a degree that people would flee, making it very difficult to keep them integrated into the system. Second, powerful bandit leaders might draw a substantial following and effectively remove those followers from the official hierarchy. On the other hand, this meant that such bandits had a following that could be readily integrated into the manpower system, since the bandits had the karmic authority associated with *nai*. The force they had at their disposal could be made to do the work of the government, provided they could be co-opted.

For the central government, co-optation was the optimal strategy. By this means, not only would the bandits end, or at least reduce, their depredations, but they also added their followers to the manpower system, and they could be used to keep the peace locally.[41] Once co-opted, the very resources that had made them a problem—a following, popular support, and the capacity and willingness to use violence—made them pillars of the local administration.

Damrong refers to this as the policy of "using thieves to catch thieves," because co-opted bandits were often used to restore order to an area by subduing rival gangs. He points out that while such arrangements could be successful at reducing banditry in the bandit's own area, it simply encouraged them secretly to shift their criminal

---

[39] See ร. ๕ รล-กห ๗๐/๑๑๖ for instance.

[40] These gangs were bound together through the enactment of magical rituals and oaths. They were formed along lines of personalistic ties, and at least some seem to have had elaborate and well-developed organizations. For a thorough account of their organization, recruitment, practices, and rituals, see สมเด็จพระเจ้าบรมวงศ์เธอ กรมพระยาดำรงราชานุภาพ, "เรื่องสนทนากับผู้ร้ายปล้น" in *วารสารเทศาภิบาล* ล. ๑ แผ่นที่ ๑ [Prince Damrong Rajanubhab, "Conversation with a Bandit" in *Thesaphiban Journal*, vol. 1, #1], pp. 17-67. An edited, condensed version is available in his *นิทานโบราณคดี* [*Historical Tales*] (Bangkok: Samnakphim Khlangwithaya, BE 2517), pp. 180-90. See also David Bruce Johnston, "Bandit, *Nakleng* and Peasant in Rural Thai Society," *Contributions to Asian Studies* 15 (1980), pp. 90-101.

[41] คมเนตร ญาณโสภณ, "อำนาจท้องถิ่นแบบจารีตและผลกระทบจากการเปลี่ยนแปลงการปกครอง ท้องถิ่นในยุคเทศาภิบาล" [Khomnet Yansophon, "Traditional Local Power and the Impact of the Change of Local Administration in the Thesaphiban Period"] (MA Thesis in the Faculty of Arts, Thammasat University, BE 2534), p. 116.

activity to nearby areas.[42] In Ayuthaya, for instance, the local *cao* appointed a bandit to keep the peace, with the result that there was very little crime against locals, but a great deal against travelers.[43] The connection between bandits and the government also worked the other way around: *nai* would sometimes turn to crime, and in the absence of any other local power, they could operate virtually unchecked.[44]

When banditry grew so troublesome that officials worried their *phrai* might start migrating from the area or that tax collection would be disrupted, the central government would send out a royal commissioner[45] to assist the local *cao* in suppressing the problem. This official would draft the manpower he needed locally and attempt to hunt down the worst offenders.[46] Such efforts met with varying degrees of success, but overall most villagers probably saw their own local gangs as more reliable protection against bandits than either the local or the central government.[47]

Religion

Monks could wield a great deal of power locally. They could influence opinion through a reputation for wisdom or learning, or they might acquire a following more directly by developing a reputation for magical powers which they could use to reward or threaten villagers. In either case, a good reputation could bring a monk a considerable lay following, and thus—in terms of the old system—a great deal of power.

Normally such monks would be integrated into the local power structure. *Nai* would patronize them and make them offerings, in return for their magical assistance and advice. Thus the monk and his following could be integrated relatively harmoniously into local politics. Bandits also often had connections with famous monks and might circulate stories that these monks had taught them magic or given them talismans to make them invulnerable. The monks might also circulate such stories, which enhanced their own reputation for magic.

Monks seldom challenged the local government directly. There was relatively little reason or opportunity to do so. The central government and the Bangkok clergy had very little control over the local clergy prior to the Sangha reform of 1902, and unorthodox beliefs were widespread. Indeed, Craig Reynolds has noted that Bangkok faced many of the same problems in appointing abbots to monasteries outside Bangkok that it faced appointing local government officials.[48] Since the

---

[42] ดำรง, *เทศาภิบาล* [Damrong, *Thesaphiban*], pp. 27-9.

[43] William J. Siffin, *The Thai Bureaucracy: Institutional Change and Development* (Honolulu: East-West Center, 1966), p. 67.

[44] See for instance ร. ๕ รล-กห ๗๐/๑๑๒.

[45] The Thai term is *kha luang* (ข้าหลวง).

[46] See for instance ร. ๕ รล-มท ๑๖/๑๖๕ and ๑๖๖ (pp. 351-3).

[47] Johnston, "Rural Society and the Rice Economy," p. 140; คมเนตร, "อำนาจท้องถิ่นแบบจารีต" [Khomnet, "Traditional Local Power"], pp. 78, 112. Khomnet goes so far as to say that the central government had no policy at all of exercising its power to protect people at the level of the village. See especially p. 3.

[48] Craig J. Reynolds, "The Buddhist Monkhood in Nineteenth-Century Thailand" (PhD Dissertation, Cornell University, 1972), p. 212.

Sangha was decentralized prior to the reforms of the Fifth Reign, there was no official dogma; heterodoxy was not an issue, because there was no orthodoxy.

As with bandits, the central government stirred itself to deal with renegade monks only on an ad hoc basis, when they were forced to. This happened when religious figures began to collect substantial followings, incite violence, or make claims that threatened the king's position as defender of the faith and the most meritorious person in the kingdom.

Most of the organized opposition to the old system seems to have taken the form of religious movements focused around "holy men" (*phu mi bun*). The central government was more sensitive to such religious movements than to banditry. Because of the scholarship of Tej Bunnag, Charles Keyes, and John Murdoch on the Holy Men rebellions of 1901-2 in the Northeast, this type of revolt is often interpreted as a reaction to political change and modernity. In fact, there was a long tradition of such revolts. Nonglak's study of rebellion in the Northeast begins with the Ay Chiang Kaew revolt of 1791 (RS 9), at the very beginning of the Chakri dynasty.[49] There was another such incident in Nakhon Ratchasima in the Third Reign.[50] One Fourth Reign proclamation mentions a "magician" (*phu wiset*) who "interfered" in the politics of his town. Another concerns a *phu mi bun* rebellion in the Northeast.[51] Chatthip Nartsupha discusses an Ayuthaya period revolt of 1699, and then traces a long history of such revolts, with the last in 1959.[52] Thus, such incidents recurred throughout the early Bangkok period, as well as both before and after. They appear to be less a function of political change than a persistent feature of the traditional political culture. In a system where power is conceptually linked to karma, and where monks are by definition karmically superior, monks will tend to become politically powerful. This tendency is limited by the fact that the karmic authority of monks is generated by their renunciation of the world, and hence depends upon them not appearing to seek power. However, monks could and did become focal points for local resistance to the higher levels of government.

---

[49] นงลักษณ์ ลิ้มศิริ, "ความสำคัญของกบฏหัวเมืองอีสาน พศ ๒๓๒๕ - ๒๔๔๕" [Nonglak Limsiri, "The Significance of the Rebellions in the Northeastern Provinces of Thailand BE 2325 – 2445"] (MA in History, Chulalongkorn University, BE 2524).

[50] จดหมายเหตุนครราชสีมา [*Documents on Nakhaun Ratchasima*] (Bangkok: Fine Arts Department, BE 2497), pp. 28-33.

[51] ประภาส จารุเสถียร รวบรวม, *ประชุมประกาศ ร. 4* [Praphat Carusathian, *Collected Proclamations of the 4th Reign*], vol. 1, #141 (Bangkok: Memorial Volume for Phra Mahaphotiwongsuacan Inthachothera, BE 2511), pp. 269-70 and vol. 2, #248, pp. 142-5. In the latter case the holy men circulated millenarian tracts in Mon, Burmese, Thai and Chinese in addition, presumably, to Lao—a tribute to the multiethnic character of old Siam.

[52] Chatthip Nartsupha, "The Ideology of Holy Men Revolts in North East Thailand," in *History and Peasant Consciousness in Southeast Asia*, ed. Andrew Turton and Shigeharu Tanabe (Osaka: National Museum of Ethnography, 1984), pp. 111-134. According to Charles Keyes, the *phu mi bun* tradition was alive and well in Bangkok and the Northeast into the mid-1970s at least. Charles Keyes, "Millenarianism, Theravada Buddhism and Thai Society," *Journal of Asian Studies* 36,2 (1977): 290. See also Constance Wilson, "The Holy Man in the History of Thailand and Laos," *Journal of Southeast Asian Studies* 28,2 (1997): 345-64.

Typically a Holy Man revolt would begin after a local religious figure acquired a reputation for performing miracles, healing the sick, or providing magical protection for followers. A particularly famous religious figure might then become the object of rumors that he was somehow more than human, or that he represented a supernatural figure. This was consonant with the belief that some people were karmically superior, a belief which created a continuum between the natural and supernatural worlds, with karma imparting a kind of magical quality to the effectiveness of superiors. In fact, a Fourth Reign proclamation even refers to princes and officials of the central government as "persons of merit" —*phu mi bun*—the same term of reference for "holy men."[53]

Sometimes these religious figures would claim special status as the Maitreya Buddha or as forerunners of the Maitreya Buddha, but these movements were not always necessarily millenarian.[54] However, they often provoked a severe response from the central government. In fact, it seems that in many of these cases it was the central government that instigated violence, using force to put down movements that had been peaceful. The followers of the "holy men" often resorted to violence only after they were attacked.[55]

Why was the central government so sensitive to these religious movements? It was clearly not out of a desire to enforce religious orthodoxy. The central government took little interest in local religious affairs. Villages selected their own abbots, the monks were generally of local origin, and there was no central control over religious texts, practice, or belief.[56] The centralized and standardized Sangha of modern Thailand is a product of the reforms of the Fifth Reign. Prior to that, the central government displayed little interest in promoting religious orthodoxy.

It was also not out of a desire to maintain internal order that these movements were suppressed. Many were non-violent until the central government intervened.[57] Furthermore, the central government's negligent attitude toward banditry would seem to indicate a minimal concern for domestic tranquillity. Local leaders were usually left on their own to keep the peace as they saw fit, as long as *phrai* were not being driven away. Local officials consequently often tolerated *phu mi bun* movements; they even participated in them. From the local perspective, such movements could have many meanings. They could be expressions of protest, assertions of local autonomy, opportunities for local leaders to enhance their powers, or simply expressions of admiration for a particular religious leader.

The central government responded more forcefully because, from the court's point of view, *phu mi bun* rebellions threatened the legitimacy of the king, and by extension, that of the political order. None of these movements ever came close to

---

[53] ประภาส, *ประชุมประกาศ ร. ๔* [Praphat, *Collected Proclamations of the 4th Reign*] vol. 1, #139, pp. 261-2.

[54] The Maitreya Buddha is the Buddha of the future. His coming, indicating that this world had lapsed into the final stages of its corruption, would usher in a new golden age of virtue.

[55] นงลักษณ์, "ความสำคัญของกบฏ" [Nonglak, "Significance of the Rebellions"], p. 125.

[56] Reynolds, "Buddhist Monkhood," p. 26; คมเนตร, "อำนาจท้องถิ่นแบบจารีต" [Khomnet, "Traditional Local Power"], p. 121; Kamala Tiyavanich, *Forest Recollections: Wandering Monks in Twentieth-Century Thailand* (Honolulu: University of Hawai'i Press, 1997), pp. 23-40.

[57] นงลักษณ์, "ความสำคัญของกบฏ" [Nonglak, "Significance of the Rebellions"], pp. 105-6.

matching the power or resources of the throne, but they did pose an ideological threat. The official political theory was based on the premise that the king was the most meritorious person in the kingdom. Anyone rumored to possess a unique connection with the future Buddha, let alone claiming to be the Maitreya Buddha himself, was claiming in effect that the current age and its rulers were corrupt, and that he personally had special, supernaturally abundant stores of merit. This posed a potent ideological threat to the king and the court in the cultural context of the old system.[58] If such a movement were to spread, or even to be tolerated by the central government, that in itself would be taken as evidence of the holy man's karmic superiority. Such confirmation might allow the movement to reach truly dangerous proportions. Prompt and violent suppression of these movements at the very least had the effect of showing that the holy man's powers — which were a function of his merit — were no match for the king. The holy man's claims were thus effectively disproved.

MINORITIES

The *nai–phrai* relationship gave the old system extraordinary flexibility in dealing with minorities. Usually *phrai* were under *nai* of their own ethnicity, and they were allowed to conduct their own affairs so long as they paid their taxes and kept the peace.

There were an immense variety of different groups integrated into old Siam: Burmese, Indian, Karen, Khmer, Lao, Mon, Shan, Vietnamese, and more. In addition, there were some Europeans in Siamese employ and numerous Chinese immigrants, who were included in the system through Siamese-appointed Chinese officials.

Not only was this profusion of ethnicity not a problem in the old system, kings positively gloried in it. Proclamations sometimes began by enumerating the breadth of their jurisdiction, and they would then sometimes elaborate on the many peoples composing the kingdom. The king's authority over such a diverse polity recalled the world-conquering *chakravartin*; a king could bolster his status by emphasizing the number and variety of peoples that accepted his authority.

Relations between these various peoples seem to have been relatively harmonious. Their status was not a function of ethnicity, but rather of the group's recent history, their tax burden, and the political acumen of their *nai*. Since the system was personalistic, ethnicity was not a threat to the kingdom — the kingdom did not have a distinctively ethnic Thai character to threaten. It was only with the coming of the modern state, which connected all citizens directly to the central government, that the creation of a homogenous Thai national identity began. Two minorities deserve special mention for the peculiar treatment they received in the old system, however. They are the Chinese and the tribespeople known as *Kha*.

The Chinese in old Siam were by and large a privileged minority. In towns with large Chinese populations they practiced self-government through special Chinese

---

[58] คมเนตร, "อำนาจท้องถิ่นแบบจารีต" [Khomnet, "Traditional Local Power"], p. 131.

officials called *kromakan cin* who were supposed to keep order in the Chinese community. These officials performed this task more or less well in different places.[59]

As one might expect given the high value placed on access to manpower, the kings of the early Bangkok period encouraged immigration. The Chinese were courted through a variety of special concessions: comparatively lower taxes, freedom of movement, trading privileges, and exemption from corvée duty.[60] The Chinese were also allowed to smoke opium, which was officially forbidden to all other ethnic groups in the Fourth and Fifth Reigns.

Chinese had to wear a pigtail and pay a triennial head tax symbolized by a string tied around the wrist and attached with a special seal. This was largely a matter of self-identification: without such distinguishing marks, there would have been no way to tell immigrant Chinese apart from ordinary *phrai*.[61] Shaving the pigtail and enrolling as a *phrai* under a *nai* constituted legal entrance into the kingdom, the equivalent of declaring oneself a Siamese subject.

There was movement in both directions. Chinese became *phrai*, and some *phrai* tried to pass themselves off as Chinese. Entering the *phrai* system seems to have been a voluntary act for Chinese, although when they did so they were still designated by their ethnic origins as *cin phrai*,[62] in much the same way that Mon or Vietnamese *phrai* might also be identified by their ethnic origins. Such a move was not necessarily irreversible. One elderly Chinese man who had achieved high rank in the Siamese government petitioned to have his eldest son "who does not wear the pigtail as a Chinese and is tattooed on the wrist as a *phrai* of *meuang* Samut Prakan" restored to his previous, pigtail-wearing status.[63]

People also tried to move in the other direction. Siamese subjects would sometimes grow pigtails or wear false ones in order to pretend to be Chinese. The government usually assumed that these crossovers were motivated by a desire to gain access to opium, although the low taxes paid by the Chinese must have also provided an incentive. These people were known as *cin plaeng*, "counterfeit" or "changed" Chinese. The Siamese government was understandably unhappy with such people, because such defections constituted a potential drain on the manpower system. They therefore prescribed penalties for *phrai* pretending to be Chinese.[64]

---

[59] M. R. Rujaya Abhakorn, "Ratburi, An Inner Province: Local Government and Central Politics in Siam, 1862-1892" (PhD Dissertation, Cornell University, 1984), p. 165; ร. ๔ รล-กห ๑๖/๗๗, and ร. ๕ ม ๑.๔/๖.

[60] อัญชลี, "ระบบไพร่" [Anchalee, "Phrai System"], p. 84.

[61] On the more or less voluntary nature of this choice, see ร. ๕ ม ๒/๑๒ ป ๒/๑๘.

[62] Kasian Tejapira, "Pigtail: A Pre-History of Chineseness in Siam," *Sojourn* 7,1 (1992): 107-8, and ร. ๕ รล-พศ ๓/๖๖. Note that the normal word order is reversed, however. In Thai the modifier follows the noun, so a Vietnamese *phrai* would be referred to as *phrai Yuan*, for instance. *Cin phrai* are being identified as Chinese most importantly, modified by the unusual circumstance of being *phrai*.

[63] ร. ๕ ม ๑.๔/๖.

[64] Kasian, "Pigtail," p. 113, who translates *cin plaeng* as "fake Chinese," and ร. ๔ รล-กห ๑๖/๗๗.

Another way Chinese removed themselves from the system was through joining secret societies or *angyi*.[65] These organizations created ongoing difficulties for the Siamese, particularly in the South. They were perceived by the central government to be the instigators of unrest among the tin miners there, most notably during the riots in Phuket in the late Fourth and early Fifth Reigns.[66]

The Chinese were useful to the central government precisely because they were not part of the manpower system. The Chinese were aliens, not really a part of the kingdom, but as merchants and hired laborers they provided useful services which could not be articulated within the *nai-phrai* relationship that bound most Siamese. Chinese merchants depended on the court for their privileges, but their activities provided the court with additional revenues. Chinese workers provided a more reliable source of labor than *phrai* serving corvée; although they cost cash money to hire, they would not leave their work without notice as *phrai* might.[67]

The peculiar status of the Chinese as aliens integrated into the political system is highlighted by the fact that special Chinese courts, with Chinese judges, were created by the Siamese. These were much like the consular courts created for European subjects under the extraterritoriality provisions of Siam's various treaties, except that the Chinese were not entitled to them by any treaty rights.[68] The central government simply found it more convenient to separate conflicts within the Chinese community from the regular legal system. The districts with the highest concentration of Chinese had officials, also appointed by the Siamese, called *kongsun cin*—"Chinese consuls." These officials were expected to keep order within the Chinese community much as European consuls were responsible for their nationals.[69]

Not all minorities were as privileged as the Chinese. Most Southeast Asians— Mon, Khmer, Lao, Cham, and Malay—were treated like any other *phrai*. Hilltribe groups were integrated into the system through *nai* who were normally of the same ethnicity, but might be Siamese or Lao. At the bottom of the hierarchy came the primitive tribal groups of the North and Northeast known collectively as *Kha*.

According to Murdoch, "'Kha' is the common, though somewhat pejorative, term used for the Austro-Asiatic tribal people of Northeast Thailand, Laos, and Vietnam."[70] Mayoury and Pheuiphanh include similar Austronesian groups in the category as well.[71] The term is generic, used for a number of groups with a very low level of technological and political sophistication. These groups of people were dependent on the Lao and Siamese, who regarded them as barely human. Both the

---

[65] ร. ๕ ม ๒.๑๒ ก/๓.

[66] ดำรง, *นิทานโบราณคดี* [Damrong, *Historical Tales*], pp. 267-9, 273-80.

[67] On the usefulness of the Chinese to the Chakri kings, see G. William Skinner, *Chinese Society in Thailand: An Analytical History* (Ithaca: Cornell University Press, 1957), p. 97. Skinner estimates that nearly half the royal revenue of the early Bangkok period kings was derived directly or indirectly from the Chinese. See especially p. 125.

[68] ดำรง, *นิทานโบราณคดี* [Damrong, *Historical Tales*], p. 271.

[69] Ibid., p. 272. Many Chinese, however, registered as foreign protégés in order to evade Siamese taxation altogether. Skinner, *Chinese Society in Thailand*, pp. 145-7.

[70] Murdoch, "1901-2 'Holy Man's' Rebellion," p. 8.

[71] Mayoury Ngaosyvathn and Pheuiphanh Ngaosyvathn, *Paths to Conflagration: Fifty Years of Diplomacy and Warfare in Laos, Thailand, and Vietnam, 1778-1828* (Ithaca: Cornell Southeast Asia Program Publications, 1998), p. 47, note 9.

Lao and Siamese conducted slaving expeditions against them in the nineteenth century. When they were integrated into the kingdom, it was always through Lao or Siamese masters.[72]

This history of abuse provoked a series of rebellions against both the Lao and the Siamese. The 1901-2 "Holy Men's" Rebellion originated among these people. Because of their lowly status, the *Kha* were highly vulnerable to change under the old system. Dependent on, and oppressed by, the Siamese and Lao, the *Kha* were most threatened by the reforms of King Chulalongkorn.

The *Kha* and the Chinese were both exceptional groups, however, representing extremes in our discussion of the Siamese Kingdom's integration of minorities. Both were integrated into the Kingdom through special means — the *Kha* through Siamese and Lao masters on terms much worse than those offered ordinary *phrai*, the Chinese through Siamese-appointed Chinese officials. Yet neither group illustrates the conditions encountered generally by minorities in Old Siam, since most minorities in the Kingdom were integrated through *nai* on terms more or less the same as Siamese. They would be registered to *nai*, often of their own ethnicity, and treated as ordinary *phrai*.

Aside from exceptional minority groups, such as the *Kha* and the Chinese, the vast majority of people in Siam were integrated into the official hierarchy as *nai*, *phrai*, or *that*. It was on the foundation of these personalistic ties that higher-level political institutions were built.

---

[72] นงลักษณ์, "ความสำคัญของกบฏ" [Nonglak, "Significance of the Rebellions"], pp. 52-3, and Holt Hallett, *A Thousand Miles On An Elephant in the Shan States* (London: William Blackwood & Sons, 1890), pp. 22-3. The word *kha* is actually the Lao word for servant.

Chapter 4

POLITICAL INSTITUTIONS: PROVINCIAL AND CENTRAL GOVERNMENT

Grassroots relationships between local leaders and followers were the basic building blocks from which the higher levels of government were constructed. Officials at higher levels of government understood and respected those foundational relationships. While they may have wished they could control local officials more closely, in practice they had to operate in ways that prudence, experience, and their schemata for political life dictated.

Since the Siamese concept of power was grounded in the assumption that an official's personal authority over followers indicated his karmic status, the higher levels of government were forced to delegate power to local leaders. The officials of the central or even provincial governments could not personally maintain relationships with all the *phrai* in the kingdom. Instead, they chose a second-best strategy of cultivating personal relationships with *nai*, creating a pyramid of power that channeled resources to the higher levels of government. In this hierarchy, the recognition of status benefited both superior and inferior. Intermediate officials benefited because their authority over their followers was legitimated by recognition from above, while their superiors benefited through the submission of powerful clients. This hierarchy could mobilize considerable resources, but it always had to respect the interests of local officials in managing their *phrai*.

CAO MEUANG AND KROMAKAN

Intermediate between the capital and the local level was the *meuang*. Like the term *phrai*, *meuang* is difficult to translate into English. It can be used to refer to a town, and this is how it is generally translated. Another common translation is "province." The problem with both translations is that they refer to clearly bounded geographical entities, while *meuang* is geographically ambiguous. It can refer to a town, but it can also refer to a country, as in the common expression *meuang Thai* for Thailand. Towns can be referred to by other terms. Large towns might be called *nakhaun*, for instance, the Thai version of the Sanskrit *nagara*. Capitals are referred to as *krung*, as in *Krungthep*, the Thai name for Bangkok, but *krung* might also refer to kingdoms or countries. These all denote a political community, not a territory per se.[1]

---

[1] *Krung* can refer to both a city, as in *Krungthep* (Bangkok), or to an entire country, as in *Krung Ratsia* (Russia) and *Krung Yipun* (Japan) cited in "ประกาศเป็นกลางในระหว่างกรุงรุสเซีย แลญี่ปุ่นทำศึกสงครามกัน" ["Decree of Neutrality in the War Between Russia and Japan"], in

As with the *nai*, the *meuang* was an institution based on personalistic ties and personal loyalties. The Siamese court considered a town deserted if there were no officials to connect it with the higher levels of government, and with good reason: lacking such intermediate officials, any town was a lacuna to them.[2] The traditional political culture required hierarchical structure to constitute authority and power; without hierarchy people could not be understood to form a significant part of the political community.

A *meuang* was not bureaucratically subdivided, nor were its functions specific. It had a geographical center in a town, but this was almost incidental; in a system based on the control of people, it was logical to locate administrative centers wherever one found the greatest population densities.[3] There were seldom any buildings specifically dedicated to the business of the *meuang*; the officers of the *meuang* simply worked out of their homes. When an office changed hands, its functions were moved to the home of the new official, even if it were not in the town.[4]

Non-territoriality

Bangkok officials often were unsure where towns were located exactly,[5] and the borders between them were defined vaguely when they were defined at all. The border between Saiburi (Kedah) and Phalit (Perlis) in the South, for instance, was defined in one place by "two papaya trees."[6] Breazeale claims that the *meuang* of Uthen in the Northeast existed for years without any territory at all—it simply consisted of settlements scattered across two other *meuang*.[7]

When the Fifth Reign reforms required rigidly demarcated boundaries, these ambiguities produced a great deal of friction between *meuang*. Most cases were dealt with by assembling a committee of representatives from each town to agree on the

---

เสถียร ลายลักษณ์ และคนอื่นๆ รวบรวม, *ประชุมกฎหมายประจำศก* [Sathian Lailak et al., eds., *Collected Laws*] vol. 19 (Bangkok: Daily Mail Printing House, BE 2478), pp. 94-5. Countries are sometimes referred to by the name of their capital as well, giving rise, for instance, to the interesting locution *prathet Bangkauk ni* (this country of Bangkok) in ร. ๕ รล ๑/๑.

[2] Kennon Breazeale, "The Integration of the Lao States into the Thai Kingdom" (PhD Dissertation, Oxford University, 1975), p. 45.

[3] Larry Sternstein has noted that every town with a population of more than five thousand in the mid-nineteenth century was a major administrative center, with populations of dependent *meuang* ranging between five hundred to three thousand people. See Larry Sternstein, "The Distribution of Thai Centres at Mid-Nineteenth Century," *Journal of Southeast Asian History* 7,1 (1966): 67.

[4] สมเด็จพระเจ้าบรมวงศ์เธอ กรมพระยาดำรงราชานุภาพ, *เทศาภิบาล* [Prince Damrong Rajanubhab, *Thesaphiban*] (Bangkok: Memorial Volume for *Phraya* Atkrawisunthon, BE 2503), pp. 26-7.

[5] James Fitzroy McCarthy, *Surveying and Exploring in Siam* (London: John Murray, 1900), p. 18; and Thongchai Winichakul, *Siam Mapped: A History of the Geo-Body of a Nation* (Honolulu: University of Hawai'i Press, 1994), pp. 30-1.

[6] ร. ๕ ม. ๒.๑๒ก ใบบอกนครศรีธรรมราช ๑/๒. This provoked trouble in the Fifth Reign when it became necessary to mark the administrative boundaries; no one remembered which trees were supposed to be the markers.

[7] Breazeale, "Integration of the Lao States," p. 47.

border. Some cases were quite complex. One such dispute is particularly well preserved in the historical record because it also involved marking the border between two larger administrative units, and it eventually had to be decided by the king. The details of this case illustrate nicely the problem of conceiving of *meuang* as geographical entities.

The *meuang* of Thak and Thoen coexisted in the same region more or less peacefully until a dispute arose in the nineteenth century over timber rights. These had become important because European-owned timber companies were expanding their operations and would pay the *meuang* officials substantial sums for the right to cut timber in what the Europeans understood to be the *meuang's* exclusive area of jurisdiction. Both Thak and Thoen made representations to the Ministry of the Interior claiming rights to the forest in question. Officials of Thoen pointed out that their *meuang* was mentioned in ancient chronicles as controlling the area, that people from Thoen had founded a village there, and that its officials had suppressed banditry and assigned logging rights to local foresters, sending some of the logs to Bangkok as *suai* (tax payment in kind, not cash). Officials of Thak, on the other hand, noted that they had been assigned by the capital to collect duties in three districts in the area. Settlers from Thak had also founded villages there, and Thak still administered those villages.

In other words, until the timber dispute arose, these two *meuang* had in effect overlapped. Both administered villages in the area and carried out special functions and police duties there: corvée timber, toll and duty collection, and the suppression of banditry. Indeed, the fact that Thak had never complained about Thoen cutting timber there before suggests that timber rights per se were not the issue, but rather Bangkok's new policy of drawing precise borders between *meuang*. This policy turned timber revenues into a zero-sum game, whereas before they had been a shared resource.[8]

Prior to the creation of territorially distinct provinces, *meuang* were not geographically well-defined. Their functions, duties, and resources could overlap. While a *meuang* existed in a particular place, the place did not define it—what was important and defined the *meuang* were the people who composed it. The fact that those people happened to live on a particular piece of land was almost coincidental.

Land within the *meuang* was not carefully mapped out either. Periodic assessments were made for the rice tax, but it was the crop that mattered, and little importance was attached to the land itself. No maps were made or records of land

---

[8] ร. ๕ ม ๒.๑/๑๕. Lest it be thought that this is a peculiarity of the sparsely populated Northwest, Piyachat and Theerachai both note the same phenomenon in the Northeast. See ปิยะฉัตร ปิตะวรรณ, *ระบบไพร่ในสังคมไทย พศ ๒๔๑๑ - ๒๔๕๓* [Piyachat Pitawan, *The Phrai System in Thai Society BE 2411 - 2453*] (Bangkok, Thammasat University, BE 2526), pp. 65-6 and ธีรชัย บุญมาธรรม, "ประวัติศาสตร์ท้องถิ่นของหัวเมืองกาฬสินธุ์ พศ ๒๓๓๖ - ๒๔๕๐" [Theerachai Boonmathum, "A Local History of Huamuang Kalasin, 1793 - 1907"] (MA Thesis in History, Chulalongkorn University, BE 2528), p. 194. So does Khomnet, who focuses on the Central Plains. See คมเนตร ญาณโสภณ, "อำนาจท้องถิ่นแบบจารีตและผลกระทบจากการเปลี่ยนแปลงการปกครองท้องถิ่นในยุคเทศาภิบาล" [Khomnet Yansophon, "Traditional Local Power and the Impact of the Change of Local Administration in the Thesaphiban Period"] (MA Thesis in the Faculty of Arts, Thammasat University, BE 2534), p. 140.

transfers kept, and title deeds, such as they were, were really tax receipts. Land was important only in that it was farmed by someone who paid taxes on the produce. Non-productive land was not taxed and no records were kept of it. Land was only valuable if and when it was worked, and people could generally claim as much as they could cultivate.[9]

Meuang not only overlapped, but some even had multiple sovereigns.[10] When James McCarthy, the first head of the Royal Survey Department, was dispatched to the North in the early 1890s with the aim of marking the international border, he encountered constant frustrations in trying to determine where one *meuang* ended and another began. For instance, at one point "the two head-men came to me, and were very polite, but told me that M. Tum belonged to Chieng Tung. I explained that I was merely enquiring about the boundary. They again informed me that M. Tum belonged to Siam."[11]

Local borders were not sanctioned by the central government. They were a matter of local concern. The border of the kingdom was the farthest *meuang* it controlled, but the demarcation of the border was of little concern except where roads and waterways connected *meuang*, and often not even then. They were important primarily where customs posts were erected to monitor traffic and extract taxes from passing merchants. Borders did not necessarily meet. If relations were poor, large uninhabited areas of no-man's land might be left between *meuang* or kingdoms.[12] This was in part due to competition for *phrai*: kingdoms might actually engage in a policy of depopulation, moving people or even whole *meuang* into more central areas where they would be less subject to raids.[13]

Thus the Siamese were somewhat casual about defining borders until the middle of the nineteenth century when they began to realize the fascination borders held for Europeans. Europeans were often puzzled by the Siamese attitude. When Burney inquired about the Siam-Burma border in the Third Reign, he was told to go ask old people living in the area where it was. When he pressed the issue, the court became increasingly annoyed.[14] The British also agonized for years over the cession of Penang and Wellesly Island to them by the Sultan of Saiburi (Kedah), because it was

---

[9] J. Homan van der Heide, "The Economical Development of Siam During the Last Half-Century," *Journal of the Siam Society* 3,2 (1906): 77; and David Bruce Johnston, "Rural Society and the Rice Economy in Thailand, 1880-1930" (PhD Dissertation, Yale University, 1975), p. 121. The constraint then was how much one could work. As Bowie points out, preparing new fields required capital, which advantaged wealthy households. Katherine Ann Bowie, "Peasant Perspectives on the Political Economy of the Northern Thai Kingdom of Chiang Mai in the Nineteenth Century" (PhD Dissertation, University of Chicago, 1988), p. 86.

[10] Thongchai, *Siam Mapped*, pp. 84-94. Vientiane and many of the small *meuang* in what is now Laos, for instance, paid tribute to both Siam and Vietnam. Breazeale, "Integration of the Lao States," pp. 6, 12.

[11] Anonymous, *An Englishman's Siamese Journals, 1890-1893* (Bangkok: Siam Media International, no date [1895]), p. 37. Thongchai points out that the author is clearly James Fitzroy McCarthy, since the text is virtually identical to McCarthy, *Surveying and Exploring*. See Thongchai, *Siam Mapped*, p. 119, note 27.

[12] Thongchai, *Siam Mapped*, pp. 75-8.

[13] Such a policy was carried out along the east bank of the Mekong river in the Third and Fourth reigns because of hostilities with the Vietnamese, for instance. See Snit Snuckarn and Kennon Breazeale, *A Culture in Search of Survival: The Phuan of Thailand and Laos* (New Haven: Yale Southeast Asian Studies, 1988); and Breazeale, "Integration of the Lao States," pp. 20-31.

[14] Thongchai, *Siam Mapped*, pp. 64-5.

done before the British realized he was a tributary to Bangkok. Anxious that the Siamese would raise this as a diplomatic issue, the British were firmly in the wrong. Bangkok, however, displayed little interest in the affair.[15]

Such attitudes persisted until well into the Fifth Reign. It was only when the reformers drew borders and changed the political roles of local officials that their traditional attitudes began to erode. In the traditional Siamese political culture, power was not conceived of as territorially bounded. It was only with the adoption of institutions founded on European political culture that boundaries became politically important.

Political Order

What really defined a *meuang* was a group of people organized into a certain set of hierarchical relationships through personalistic ties. The specific details of *meuang* governance varied across the kingdom, but in all cases it involved certain basic roles and relationships. There were always a group of important local officials and *nai* called *kromakan*. Most prominent among these was a group of four or five officers, appointed by the king from among local candidates, who formed in theory a kind of *cursus honorem* culminating in the office of the chief of the *meuang* (*cao meuang*). Just as the *nai* was the point of contact between the government and the *phrai*, so were the *cao meuang* and the *kromakan* the point of contact between the *nai* and the capital. The central government would send orders to the *cao meuang* and the most important *kromakan*, and they were responsible for organizing the appropriate action and delegating tasks. This emphasis on office obscures a central feature of the system, however. Those officials were usually the most important *nai* of the *meuang*. They were not powerful because of the office so much as they were appointed to the office because they had personal connections—both to superiors and inferiors—that enabled them to carry out its duties effectively. These connections were understood as a function of birth, and ultimately, of karma. Whereas in a modern bureaucratic organization an official's bureaucratic identity is defined by the office he or she holds, in the old Siamese system the official's identity—age, sex, birth, connections, and so on—defined what role he or she was suited for.

Many of the same limitations and strategies that operated in the *nai-phrai* relationship also functioned in the politics of the *meuang*. The *cao meuang* and *kromakan* were usually directly involved in the control of at least some *phrai*, and so tended to have good information about them. There would also be a number of other *nai* in the *meuang*, some under the direct control of *meuang* officials and some under the control of officials in the capital.[16] *Meuang* officials had to act as good patrons in order to keep their own clients, both *phrai* and other *nai*, happy enough to cooperate with them. The *meuang* officials might therefore choose to frustrate the wishes of the central government in the interests of local politics.[17]

---

[15] Ibid., pp. 69-70.

[16] Most *meuang* had units called *krom satsadi* charged with keeping track of the manpower rolls of the *meuang*, a function which corresponded to that of *Krom* Phrasurasawadi in the capital.

[17] This seems to be what is going on in ร. ๕ รล-กห ๗๐/๒, where central government officials complain that local officials have been "unenthusiastic" in assisting them to capture a local *nai* accused of a crime.

The central government theoretically appointed the *cao meuang* and the more important *kromakan*. In fact, it often had few candidates to choose from. Local elites had advantages in controlling both *nai* and *phrai* that an appointee from the central government could never match. They knew the people personally, had good information about them, knew local conditions, and had the right connections. Officials in the capital hoped there would be a number of possible candidates for the more important positions in the *meuang*, so that it could play them off against each other. Often there was only one candidate, however.[18] Sometimes local officials would suggest a candidate. Sometimes they were asked. They were always at least consulted.[19]

A Fourth Reign letter explains why such consultations with local officials were important: " . . . so that there will be no rancor or conflict that will harm the affairs of the kingdom in any way."[20] If the person favored by the local *nai* were passed over, he could use his connections and influence to make it impossible for the new appointee to function. Active interference was possible, but simply withholding aid and information might be enough to disrupt local government. Dismissing *meuang* officials was equally difficult for similar reasons—replacements would probably not be able to function in the face of local opposition.[21]

Attempts to force local populations to accept Bangkok's candidates as *meuang* officials were problematic. Often the central government had to accept candidates with histories of rebellion. A case in point is Kedah on the Malay peninsula, called Saiburi by the Thais. In the Second Reign the Siamese conquered this port and replaced the Malay sultan with a Siamese official. This led to a long series of revolts by partisans of the old sultan. Bangkok tried dividing the *meuang* into three parts and appointing a Malay *cao meuang* to each. This did not end the revolts, though, and in 1841, after nearly ten years, an accommodation was reached whereby the sultan was reinstated as *cao meuang* by the Thais, but under Siamese suzerainty.[22] In the most important administrative center of the South, Nakhon Si Thammarat, King Taksin deposed the ruling family for rebellion and then immediately reinstated it.[23] In the

---

[18] Tej Bunnag, *The Provincial Administration of Siam, 1892-1915: the Ministry of the Interior Under Prince Damrong Rajanubhab* (New York: Oxford University Press, 1977), p. 19.

[19] See for instance จดหมายเหตุ ร. ๔ ๑๒๑๔/๒๓, ๒๕, ๑๒๒๐/๑๗, ๑๙, ร. ๕ รล-กห ๑๙/๒๔, ๖๙/๑๙, ม ๒.๑๒ก แผนกปกครอง (ใบบอก) นครราชสีมา ล. ๑ ปีกที่ ๑ suggests a replacement for an important local official before he was even dead. ปีกที่ ๒ recommends the son of the *cao meuang* as a replacement for the position of *yokkrabat*, an official that Akin claims was supposed to act as a "spy" for the king. Akin Rabibhadana, *The Organization of Thai Society in the Early Bangkok Period, 1782-1873* (Ithaca: Cornell Southeast Asia Program, 1969), p. 71.

[20] จดหมายเหตุ ร. ๔ ๑๒๒๐/๑๙.

[21] Tej, *Provincial Administration*, p. 29. McCarthy gives an example of such a case in one of the Northern tributary states in *Surveying and Exploring*, p. 103.

[22] Walter Vella, *Siam Under Rama III, 1824-1851* (Locust Valley, NY: J. J. Augustin, 1957), pp. 75-6; อริยา เสถียรสุต, "เจ้าเมืองนครศรีธรรมราชสมัยการปกครองแบบเก่าแห่งกรุงรัตนโกสินทร์" [Ariya Sathiansut, "The Governorship of Ligor Under the Old System of Government of the Bangkok Period"] (MA Thesis in History, Chulalongkorn University, BE 2514), pp. 94-5.

[23] Tej, *Provincial Administration*, p. 19.

Northeast the regent for the *cao meuang* of Kalasin rebelled and fled to Vientiane, but was subsequently reinstated by Bangkok.[24]

The net result was that the position of *cao meuang* was largely hereditary, restricted at most to one or two prominent families. Even well into the Bangkok period many *cao* came from families that had governed their *meuang* since the Ayuthaya period.[25]

This limitation on appointing officials has often been taken to mean that Bangkok had no control over the *meuang*. *Meuang* often acted independently and succeeded in defying the court. On the other hand, it is equally clear that Bangkok possessed the means to exercise considerable control over the *meuang*, even those quite distant from the capital, when it chose to do so. It could manipulate local conflicts, send out royal commissioners, and ultimately use force against *meuang* officials. Yet the court seems to have been reluctant to exercise its power in this way, and often tolerated independence and defiance from the *meuang*.

Central Control and Local Autonomy

Bangkok's most obvious source of power over the *meuang* was the control of appointments. While local offices were largely hereditary, they did not follow any strict rule of succession. This gave Bangkok the opportunity to choose from among several possible candidates the one who seemed most likely to respect the central government. It gave the capital the capacity to exploit differences between rivals at the *meuang* level, be they among rival families, lineages of the same family, or siblings. Since the ruling families of *meuang* located near each other tended to be interrelated, this provided an opportunity to play *meuang* off against each other as well. Local conflicts could even result in one faction leading its followers to go found another town somewhere else, the corporate version of the flight of individual *phrai*, allowing the central government to employ a policy of divide-and-rule.[26] Where local conflicts were most fierce, the capital was most powerful.[27]

The central government could also exercise its power by declining to appoint anyone to an office. In one town in the Northeast, for instance, all four major officers

---

[24] อัญชลี สุสายัณห์, "ความเปลี่ยนแปลงของระบบไพร่และผลกระทบต่อสังคมไทยในรัชสมัยพระบาทสมเด็จพระจุลจอมเกล้าเจ้าอยู่หัว [Anchalee Susayanha, "Changes of the Phrai System and their Effects on Thai Society in the Reign of King Chulalongkorn"] (MA Thesis in History, Chulalongkorn University, BE 2524), pp. 62-3.

[25] Michael Vickery, "Thai Regional Elites and the Reforms of King Chulalongkorn," *Journal of Asian Studies* 29,4 (1970): 866-8.

[26] Factions of *meuang* Kalasin, for instance, decamped to found *meuang* Kamalasai and *meuang* Sahatsakhon. ธีรชัย, "กาฬสินธุ์" [Theerachai, "Kalasin"], Chapter 4. On this policy of divide-and-rule as it applied to the Lao *meuang*, see Mayoury Ngaosyvathn and Pheuiphanh Ngaosyvathn, *Paths to Conflagration: Fifty Years of Diplomacy and Warfare in Laos, Thailand and Vietnam, 1778-1828* (Ithaca: Cornell Southeast Asia Program, 1998), pp. 43-4.

[27] คมเนตร, "อำนาจท้องถิ่นแบบจารีต" [Khomnet, "Traditional Local Power"], p. 46.

were allowed to die off without being replaced, so that the *meuang* could then be merged with another one.[28]

There were also a variety of titles Bangkok could confer on local officials, each carrying subtly different powers and privileges. Along with certain titles would go specific rights, such as the right to collect certain taxes, to keep certain revenues or goods for private use, or to maintain control over certain groups of *phrai*. These titles could also be used as incentives to *meuang* officials to cooperate with the center.

In the Third Reign, Bangkok began appointing tax farmers, primarily to the *meuang* of the Central Plains and the South.[29] Typically these would be Chinese merchants who had identified industries that might support a tax and had proposed the farm to the court. An auction would then be held at which the highest bidder would be awarded the farm.

The effect of tax farming was to improve dramatically Bangkok's control over taxation in the *meuang*.[30] The tax farmers also had certain police powers attached to their farms, such as interdicting smugglers and bootleggers and checking illegal gambling. All this meant that they were somewhat at odds with the existing system of administration and were potential rivals to the other officials of the *meuang*. It took time for the two groups to learn to accommodate each other. According to Hong,

> The instances of conflict that occurred between the tax farmers, representatives of the king's interests, and the local authorities centred on the view that the farmers were intruders on the local scene who undermined the power and privileges of the provincial magnates. The latter refused to succumb to the encroachment and resisted by defying the powers that the tax farmers were invested with. Where such a hostile situation existed, the most the tax farmer could do was to collect the taxes according to the prescribed rates. There was little leeway for him to overtax the people if the provincial officials had more to gain from siding with the local population.
>
> The sympathies and interests of the governors, however, could be, and were often swayed by enticements from the tax farmers. When the farmer demonstrably convinced the provincial leaders that a profitable relationship could be struck between them, his work was much facilitated, mostly at the expense of the tax payers.[31]

Thus, tax farmers and local officials eventually learned to cooperate. This had the effect of undermining much of the additional leverage the central government had initially gained from tax farming.

If local officials behaved in ways that the central government did not like, there was always the possibility of recourse to law. The law codes were draconian, with the result that the king could impose virtually any penalty he liked in most cases.

---

[28] ธีรชัย, "กาฬสินธุ์" [Theerachai, "Kalasin"], p. 204. During the Fifth Reign reforms, this was to become an important tool for reducing local opposition to political change.

[29] Breazeale notes that there were no tax farmers in the Northeast except in the chief administrative center, Nakhaun Ratchasima. See Breazeale, "Integration of the Lao States," p. 93. They seem to have been uncommon in the North as well.

[30] Hong Lysa, "The Tax-Farming System in the Early Bangkok Period," *Journal of Southeast Asian Studies* 14,2 (1983): 385.

[31] Ibid., p. 392.

Generally the king's punishment would be more lenient than the maximum punishment prescribed by law, which had the additional benefit of demonstrating the king's mercy. Local officials were at least sometimes punished in response to the petitions of oppressed *phrai*.[32]

Bangkok's ultimate sanction was, however, the use of military force. Despite the slowness and difficulty of travel, Bangkok could and did mount effective campaigns even in remote areas. King Taksin restored the Ayuthaya empire through force as much as persuasion, and Rama I and II were constantly at war consolidating this conquest and defending it from the Burmese and Vietnamese. Rama III and IV mounted effective campaigns in the far north, compelling mass migrations from distant *meuang* such as Chiang Rung and Phuan.[33] Rama III also mounted a devastating campaign against Vientiane, razing the city.[34]

The result of all these tools was that the king at Bangkok held a great deal of power he could use to manipulate the *meuang*. He approved appointments even for distant tributary states[35] and conscripted troops from them.[36] According to Mayoury and Pheuiphanh, the kings of Bangkok even prevented their tributaries from manufacturing weapons.[37] As we will see below, the king also had the authority to alter institutions. The question then is this: if the king possessed this power, why had no previous king used it to rein in defiant *cao meuang* and centralize the kingdom?

The answer, I would argue, is that in the old system it was in the king's interest to permit the officials of the *meuang* wide latitude. The king could not afford to control local affairs too tightly because he lacked precise information about local conditions and geography. He needed the personalistic ties that local officials had with their *nai*, and the *nai* had in turn with their *phrai*, in order to keep them in the system. And since control over *phrai* constituted power, the king wanted to keep as many of them in the system as possible. Understood within the schemata of the traditional political culture, the king was maximizing his power by allowing local officials so much autonomy.

Meuang officials had to be allowed discretion in dealing with local *nai* and *phrai* in order to keep them in the system, and they themselves had to be induced to cooperate with the capital. Thus, they were allowed to keep some *phrai* hidden and to

---

[32] See for instance, "ประกาศว่าด้วยพระยาไชยา (กลับ)" in เสถียร, *ประชุมกฎหมาย ประจำศก* [Sathian, *Collected Laws*] vol. 6, pp. 66-70, or จดหมายเหตุ ร. ๔ ๑๒๑๓/๑๔.

[33] จดหมายเหตุ ร. ๔ ๑๒๑ ๔/๑๖, ๑๒๑๕/๑๗, ๑๒๑๖/๕๕, and also Breazeale and Snit, *Phuan*.

[34] อำมาตย์โท พระยาสากลกิจประมวญ รวบรวม, *ประชุมจดหมายเหตุเรื่องปราบกบฏเวียงจันทน์* [Amattho Phraya Sakolkitpramuan, ed. *Collected Documents on Suppressing the Wiang Chan Rebellion*] (Bangkok: Memorial Volume for Caocaummarada Maum Ratchawong Saeng, BE 2473).

[35] จดหมายเหตุ ร. ๔ ๑๒๑๔/๒๓, ๑๒๒๐/๑๗.

[36] จดหมายเหตุ ร. ๔ ๑๒๑๔/๓๔, ๑๒๑๖/๕๕.

[37] Mayoury and Pheuiphanh, *Paths to Conflagration*, p. 168. They claim in the same passage that Bangkok also prevented the Lao from maintaining a standing army. However, none of their neighbors had a standing army either, including Siam. Armies were raised as needed, and in times of peace they were disbanded. See Noel Alfred Battye, "The Military, Government and Society in Siam, 1868-1910: Politics and Military Reform During the Reign of King Chulalongkorn" (PhD Dissertation, Cornell University, 1974), pp. 10-11.

underpay taxes, and they were not required to obey central orders too precisely. They could thereby maximize the number of *phrai* under their control and therefore indirectly under Bangkok's control as well.

Royal Commissioners (Kha Luang)

One of Bangkok's most important mechanisms for keeping *meuang* officials at least moderately honest was the practice of sending out royal commissioners on an ad hoc basis, somewhat like the commissars or *intendents* of early modern Europe.[38] These were generally important officials of the court, and they were sent out on a strictly temporary basis. As we saw above, these officials might be sent to deal with a particularly outrageous banditry problem. They were also sent out periodically to conduct mass tattooings and to update the manpower rolls.

These mass tattooings were conducted at least once in every reign, to rectify the manpower rolls and also to symbolize the transfer of royal authority. An important official would be sent from Bangkok to oversee the registration of *phrai* for an entire region. Typically he would set up headquarters in one of the largest regional towns, conscript some *phrai* to work for him, and send out notices to the surrounding *meuang* ordering that all *nai* bring in their *phrai* to be registered and tattooed. After a specified period of time had elapsed, he would form patrols to comb the area to catch any *phrai* not yet tattooed. These would be registered as royal *phrai* and assigned to the *meuang*.[39] Local officials were enjoined to assist in catching unmarked *phrai* and were rewarded for each one caught.[40] *Nai* and *phrai* who were discovered to have conspired to prevent registration were threatened with dire punishments.[41]

Just as tattooing was the symbolic act by which *phrai* submitted to the central government, it was also a symbol of a *meuang*'s inclusion in the kingdom. *Meuang* in which *phrai* were tattooed were formally subordinate to Bangkok. If *phrai* were not tattooed, this was one symbol of the *meuang*'s formal independence and tributary status. Hence Rama III's extension of tattooing into the Northeast was one of the factors behind the rebellion of *Cao Anu* of Vientiane.[42]

---

[38] See Otto Hintze, "The Commissary and His Significance in General Administrative History: A Comparative Study," in *The Historical Essays of Otto Hintze*, ed. Felix Gilbert (New York: Oxford University Press, 1975), pp. 267-301.

[39] เสถียร, *ประชุมกฎหมายประจำศก* [Sathian, *Collected Laws*] vol. 9, pp. 161-2; ร. ๔ รล-กห ๑๑/๑๐๖, ๑๙/๓๕, ๔๑, จดหมายเหตุ ๑๒๑๘/๔๒, ๑๒๒๐/๕๕๒, ร. ๕ รล-กห ๒/๓๗, ๗๑/๘๐.

[40] "ประกาศให้สมเด็จเจ้าพระยาทั้ง ๒ องค์ เปนแม่กองสักเลก" ["Proclamation for both *Somdet Caophrayas* to Lead *Phrai* Tattooing Units"], in ประภาส จารุเสถียร, รวบรวม, *ประชุมประกาศ ร. ๔* [Praphat Carusathian, ed., *Collected Proclamations of the Fourth Reign*] vol. 1, #58 (Bangkok: Memorial Volume for Phra Mahaphothiwongsacan Inthachothera, BE 2511).

[41] "ประกาศโปรดให้ศักเลขไพร่หลวงหัวเมืองขึ้น และเรื่องผู้ปลอมศักเลข" ["Proclamation to Tattoo Royal *Phrai* in the *Meuang* and On Those Who Hide *Phrai*"], in เสถียร, *ประชุมกฎหมายประจำศก* [Sathian, *Collected Laws*] vol. 6, pp. 45-7.

[42] Mayoury and Pheuiphanh, *Paths to Conflagration*, pp. 144-8.

The tattooing expeditions were effective at adding unregistered *phrai* to the rolls.[43] But they could never catch everyone: there were always some unregistered *phrai*. Sometimes special policies were designed to bring in unregistered *phrai*, as when Rama III allowed fugitive *phrai* to come back into the system by choosing their own *nai*, or when Rama V promised rewards for informing on people who tried to hide *phrai*.[44] Still, there were unlimited ways to hide *phrai*. A Fifth Reign proclamation complains that heirs were even delaying the funerals of their predecessors for years in order to evade taxes on the *phrai* they inherited.[45]

In the tattooing campaigns of the Second and Third Reigns, fugitive *phrai* formally were given the freedom to choose their new *nai*.[46] In effect, though, this was usually the case.[47] *Phrai* who had fled the system and feared capture had plenty of warning and could go seek out a new *nai*.

The royal commissioners were never exclusively concerned with tattooing. They were generalists who were expected to deal with a range of other problems that might arise. When *Caophraya* Si Suriyawong was sent to conduct tattooing and registration operations in the South during the Fourth Reign, for instance, he was also asked to clear up a number of other problems: to hear commoner's complaints; recover lost *phrai*; try thirty bandits who had been terrorizing the town of Phathalung; and investigate violence between Chinese in the retinues of the *cao meuang* of Phuket and the local tin tax farmer.[48]

The Efficiency of the Old System

Modern historians have generally followed King Chulalongkorn and Prince Damrong in condemning the old Siamese political system as inefficient because of the

---

[43] For instance, one such expedition to Nakhon Ratchasima re-registered 3,489 *phrai* who were already registered and added another four thousand who were not. จดหมายเหตุ ร. ๔ ๑๒๐/๔๑.

[44] นันทิยา สว่างวุฒิธรรม, "การควบคุมกำลังคนในสมัยรัตนโกสินทร์ก่อนการจัดการเกณฑ์ทหาร (พศ ๒๓๒๕ - ๒๔๔๘)" [Nuntiya Swangvudthitham, "The Control of Manpower During the Bangkok Period Prior to the Introduction of Modern Conscription (BE 2325-2448)"] (MA Thesis in History, Chulalongkorn University, BE 2525), p. 137; and "ประกาศเลขไพร่หลวงไพร่สม, รส ๑๐๕" ["Proclamation on Royal *Phrai* and *Phrai Som*, RS 105"], in เสถียร, *ประชุมกฎหมายประจำศก* [Sathian, *Collected Laws*] vol. 11, pp. 85-6, respectively.

[45] "ประกาศเรื่องชำระเลขเจ้าสิ้นพระชนม์นายถึงแก่กรรม, รส ๑๐๖" ["Proclamation on Auditing the *Phrai* of Deceased Lords and Dead *Nai*, RS 106"], in เสถียร, *ประชุมกฎหมายประจำศก* [Sathian, *Collected Laws*] vol. 11, pp. 117-9.

[46] Lorraine Gesick, "Kingship and Political Integration in Traditional Siam" (PhD Dissertation, Cornell University, 1976), p. 176; and นันทิยา, "การควบคุมกำลังคน" [Nuntiya, "Control of Manpower"], p. 137.

[47] นันทิยา, "การควบคุมกำลังคน" [Nuntiya, "Control of Manpower"], pp. 29-30; and ธีรชัย, "กาฬสินธุ์" [Theerachai, "Kalasin"], p. 75.

[48] ร. ๔ รล-กห ๑๙/๓๕, ๔๔, ๔๗ and ๕๒, respectively.

weakness of the central government.[49] In fact, as we have seen, the central government could exercise a great deal of power when it chose. The fact that it did not often choose to is not in itself a sign of weakness; indeed, its restraint might well be interpreted as a testament to its strength.

The system was inefficient from the perspective of the modern state, but this was not the traditional Siamese perspective. The old system did not maximize the central government's ability to interfere in local affairs, but it did maximize the number of *phrai* under the ultimate control of the king. This—not the control of borders or bureaucratic efficiency—was the most important consideration in the old Siamese political culture. Strong borders and efficient officials might be desirable, but they were secondary. The primary goal of politics was to contain as many people as possible in a single hierarchy. This validated the karmic superiority of officials, and ultimately of the king, and this was the most important goal of politics according to the schemata the Siamese traditionally used to understand political life. Once introduced into the hierarchy, people could be induced to surrender time, money, or goods in kind to the higher levels of government. Given the constraints under which it operated, the old system managed this process of commanding and extracting resources effectively. Even on the eve of its demise in the 1880s, when the *phrai* system in the Central Plains was eroding badly, it could still deliver sufficient resources to King Chulalongkorn and his allies to enable them to undertake a radical reform.

This does not mean the system always operated smoothly. As in politics everywhere, problems and crises developed: individuals acted emotionally or irrationally, miscalculated or acted with insufficient information, or became locked in personality conflicts. The system described above is only an ideal type, a pattern which helps us find some order in the chaos of ordinary life. It is a reconstruction that allows us to distinguish mistakes and miscalculations from intended behaviors.

The system varied from this ideal type over time and over space. Chapter Five will address the issue of change over time. First I deal below with spatial variation: regional differences in *nai-phrai* relations and *meuang*-level organization.

Regional Variations

There were regional variations in the structure of traditional Siamese political institutions. It is primarily in the Central Plains that we find the administrative structure outlined by Akin in his classic *The Organization of Thai Society in the Early Bangkok Period*. These *meuang* generally had a gentle geography and a reliable water supply from the Caophraya river and its tributaries. Much of the land—particularly land that did not happen to front a large waterway—remained jungle or grassland well into the nineteenth century. Transportation was primarily by boat, and by all accounts the land routes were very poor.

Phrai in the Central Plains were probably better off than their counterparts elsewhere in the kingdom. While no good comparative data is available, we do know

---

[49] See for instance H. G. Quaritch Wales, *Ancient Siamese Government and Administration* (New York: Paragon, 1965 [1934]), pp. 4-5, 248; and อัญชลี, "ระบบไพร่" [Anchalee, "Phrai System"], p. 131. Akin asks us to believe the astonishing proposition that the system worked best following major crises and was eroded by long periods of peace and prosperity. Akin, *Organization of Thai Society*, p. 183.

that flight would have been a more attractive strategy in the comparatively well-watered Central Plains, because starting a new farm would have been easier than in the drier Northeast or the mountains of the North and South. In addition, the greater wealth and larger population of the Central Plains meant that there were more *nai* to choose from, if *phrai* wanted to abandon their initial *nai*. This would have probably worked to the advantage of *phrai*.

Towns in the Central Plains were more subject to the direct authority of Bangkok than those elsewhere. They were run by officials theoretically appointed by the king and were subject to his pleasure. In fact, the Inner Provinces—those closest to Bangkok—often became attached to court families on a more or less permanent basis.[50] Thus, while proximity to the capital meant that members of the court could control these provinces more effectively than the Outer Provinces, it did not follow that the king had more power over them.

The organization of the Inner Provinces paralleled that of the capital. Officially appointments were distributed among various *krom* in the capital, so that each of the capital's important *krom* had a counterpart in the *meuang*.[51] In practice, though, there was little division of labor even this close to the capital. Virtually all officials had judicial powers by the Fifth Reign.[52] If local officials were not diligent in their duty, there was little that Bangkok could do to dismiss them, even in these closest *meuang*.[53] Thus by the Fifth Reign the real difference between the Inner and Outer Provinces was that the former were ruled by court families, while the latter were ruled by a local aristocracy.

The Northeast region of the kingdom, which had the poorest soils and least rainfall, was the least suited to agriculture. It was the most sparsely populated region at the beginning of the Bangkok period. Its dominant geographical features are the Khorat Plateau and the Mekong River. Most of the people of the Northeast are ethnically Lao rather than Thai, and thus the region is culturally as well as geographically oriented to the east and the Mekong rather than to the west and the Caophraya.

The population of the Northeast increased steadily during the early Bangkok period, in part because of migration, both voluntary and involuntary, across the Mekong river. After the breakup of the Lao kingdom of Lan Chang there was a steady stream of migration across the Mekong. This accelerated in the Third and Fourth Reigns because of a policy of depopulating the river's east bank in order to deprive the Vietnamese of support for their troops in the middle Mekong region. It was also encouraged by the razing of Vientiane in the Third Reign.

In addition to compelling resettlement by force, Bangkok also tried to encourage voluntary migration. Tax burdens in the Northeast were relatively light in the early Bangkok period, and Bangkok even sent money to some of the Northeastern *meuang*

---

[50] Vickery, "Thai Regional Elites," p. 872.

[51] M. R. Rujaya Abhakorn, "Ratburi, An Inner Province: Local Government and Central Politics in Siam, 1862-1892" (PhD Dissertation, Cornell University, 1984), pp. 47, 60.

[52] Ibid., p. 115.

[53] ร. ๕ รล-กห ๗๐/๒.

to be used to assist immigrants in starting farms and buying cattle.[54] Tattooing was only introduced to the Northeast in the Third Reign.[55]

The political situation in the Northeast was quite fluid in the early Bangkok period. Lao officials were encouraged to lead their followers across the Mekong, where they would be securely under Thai suzerainty, so that they would no longer have to pay homage to both the Thai and the Vietnamese. Initially they would be attached to a *meuang*. When their settlements reached sufficient size, they could request these be made into *meuang* in their own right. The connections between *meuang* officials and *phrai* were unusually direct under these conditions, with some *meuang* having only four groups of *phrai*, each under one of the four most important local officials.[56]

The Northeast demonstrates dramatically the strength of the bonds between *nai* and *phrai*. Lao *nai* often migrated with their *phrai*, and these continued to form a coherent political unit after their arrival in Siam. The political organization of the migrants survived both a change in suzerainty and in geography. These people changed kingdoms both in the physical sense and in terms of ultimate authority, and yet their ties to their *nai* survived intact.

The *meuang* of the Northeast were organized on the Lao model rather than that of the central Thai, with the exception of the most important *meuang*, Nakhon Ratchasima. The population of the Northeast was mostly Lao and their culture derived more from the old Lao kingdom of Lan Chang than of Bangkok.[57] *Meuang* were managed by four chief officials: the *cao meuang*, *uparat*, *ratchawong*, and *ratchabut*. These officials were the most powerful *nai* in the area, and they were selected from the most powerful families.

North of the Central Plains the geography becomes more rugged, rising first into hills and then into steep mountains punctuated by level valleys suitable for growing wet rice. The geography promoted the development of a number of small, relatively independent *meuang*. These *meuang* were populated by a people whom the central Thai and most foreigners called "Lao," but the inhabitants of this region identified themselves simply as the "people of the *meuang*" (*khon meuang*). They employed a political organization similar to that of the Lao. The four major offices were the same as those described above for the Northeast. In addition, there was a council of officials, *kromakan*, and *nai*, called a *sanam luang*. Important decisions were taken by this body collectively, but the four major officials were still the most important *nai* in most cases.

Gehan Wijeyewardene argues explicitly that *meuang* did have geographical boundaries, pointing to the fact that many Northern *meuang* have shrines as

[54] ธีรชัย, "กาฬสินธุ์" [Theerachai, "Kalasin"], pp. 45, 63-4, 69, and 120-9.

[55] Ibid., pp. 57, 77-9.

[56] บุญรอด แก้วกันหา, "การเก็บส่วยในสมัยรัตนโกสินทร์ตอนต้น (พศ ๒๓๒๕ - ๒๔๑๑)" [Boonrod Keawkanha, "The Collection of Suay During the Early Ratanakosin Period (AD 1782 - 1868)"] (MA Thesis in History, Chulalongkorn University, BE 2518), p. 72.

[57] นงลักษณ์ ลิ้มศิริ, "ความสำคัญของกบฏหัวเมืองอีสาน พศ ๒๓๒๕ - ๒๔๔๕" [Nonglak Limsiri, "The Significance of the Rebellions in the Northeastern Provinces of Thailand, BE 2325 - 2445"] (MA Thesis in History, Chulalongkorn University, BE 2524), p. 30; ธีรชัย, "กาฬสินธุ์" [Theerachai, "Kalasin"], pp. 45-6.

boundary markers where the paths connecting them cross watersheds.[58] He sees the *meuang* as a

> ... river valley bounded by mountains, which was the essential unit of political community, and an ecological, agricultural unit in which the watershed and the catchment provided the irrigation for wet-rice agriculture, and the mountain passes and rivers articulated relations with the outside world.[59]

This defines the *meuang* primarily as an ecological and agricultural unit, not as a political unit. In this sense it is hardly surprising that the *meuang* formed a kind of natural unit in the North, where there are a series of relatively small mountain valleys between which travel was difficult and where watersheds and catchments are reasonably clear.[60] The fact remains, however, that as a political unit the *meuang* did not necessarily have clear borders; there are numerous cases of overlapping jurisdiction in the North, as Wijeyewardene himself admits.[61] Even in the North, where geography and ecology would most favor bounded political units, political relations were established on a personal, rather than a territorial, basis.

Because of the mountainous terrain, starting a farm in the North would have required a higher investment in labor than in the Central Plains, and the smaller population would have reduced the number of *nai* competing for *phrai*. These circumstances may have made flight a less attractive option for *phrai* in the North. This appears to be reflected in Katherine Bowie's data, gathered from interviews with elderly northerners, in which they complain bitterly of oppression under the old system.[62]

The rugged geography of the North also presented problems for the capital. In the North there were more tributaries than elsewhere in the kingdom. Even small towns such as Loei and Nan were able to maintain a measure of independence from both Bangkok and the great regional power, Chiang Mai.

On paper the Northern tributaries look more powerful and independent of Bangkok than those in the South. Many of the Northern rulers were given the title of "Lord of Life" (*Cao Chiwit*), for instance, in recognition of their assistance against *Cao Anu* in the Third Reign and in the Chiang Tung campaign of the Fourth Reign. This was a higher title than any of the tributary rulers in the South were granted, possibly a concession to the greater practical difficulties involved in overseeing the activities of the Northern *cao*. In addition, the Northerners had access to timber revenues that, in the mid-nineteenth century, temporarily gave them a financial advantage their Southern counterparts did not possess.

---

[58] Gehan Wijeyewardene, "The Frontiers of Thailand," in *National Identity and its Defenders: Thailand, 1939-1989*, ed. Craig J. Reynolds (Chiang Mai: Silkworm Books, 1991), p. 165.

[59] Ibid., p. 163. It should be noted here how little sense this kind of logic would make in the predominantly flat Central Plains, where there were seldom clear demarcations even between villages, and where most of the people in the Kingdom lived.

[60] The exception to this rule is the largest valley of the North, which supports two *meuang*: Chiang Mai and Lamphun.

[61] Ibid., p. 167.

[62] Bowie, "Peasant Perspectives." Unfortunately, it is not always clear to what period Bowie's informants are referring.

The independence of these rulers was eroded rapidly in the Fourth and early Fifth Reigns because of foreign missionaries and disputes over timber rights. These disputes divided the local elites and brought the *caos* into conflicts with foreigners, which the foreign consuls preferred to settle in Bangkok. Rama IV was able to demand rolls be drawn up of the manpower in the Northern tributaries.[63] By RS 103 (1884) the court was able to send police to the theoretically independent tributary state of Lampang to arrest the *ratchawong* and bring him back to Bangkok.[64]

The ecology of the South sets it apart from the rest of the country because it is relatively unsuited for growing rice. A mountainous spine runs down the center of the Malay peninsula; on the western side of the mountains there are only narrow coastal strips suited to rice production. On the eastern side there are larger inland valleys, but these tend to be subject to frequent and unpredictable flooding and changes in stream and river courses.[65] Even today only Nakhon Si Thammarat and Phathalung are self-sufficient in rice; all the other southern provinces depend on exports from these provinces and the Central Plains. For this reason the South in the early Bangkok period was relatively unpopulated compared to the rest of the kingdom. It did produce valuable goods, however, including tin, rubber, coconuts, and lumber.

The court sought to monopolize these goods prior to the Burney and Bowring treaties, collecting some as *suai* and purchasing the rest through local officials.[66] This economic structure, which essentially fostered production for export, was unique in the kingdom. It produced a very different political structure there, one designed to meet somewhat different goals than those of the rest of the kingdom.

Nakhaun Si Thamarat was the chief administrative center for the South, playing a role similar to that of Nakhaun Ratchasima in the Northeast. It also had a political structure more like that of the capital than any of its subordinate *meuang*. This was because it was reorganized in the Second Reign by a central government official who modeled it on the Bangkok government, giving it departments of the same name. The other *meuang* in the area were then organized as dependencies of Nakhon Si Thammarat. The system seems to have worked well, because an early Fifth Reign attempt to change it by the Regent, *Somdet Caophraya* Si Suriyawong, disappeared without a trace by the time Prince Damrong got around to inspecting the area later in the Fifth Reign. Damrong was pleased, because the older system more closely resembled the local administration he wanted to establish than had Si Suriyawong's reform.[67]

---

[63] นันทิยา, "การควบคุมกำลังคน" [Nuntiya, "Control of Manpower"], p. 26.

[64] ร. ๕ รล-มท ๒๗/๖๙.

[65] Wolf Donner, *The Five Faces of Thailand: An Economic Geography* (St. Lucia, Queensland: Queensland University Press, 1982), pp. 410, 436.

[66] Hong Lysa argues that the early Bangkok kings were less energetic about securing monopolies than their predecessors in Ayuthaya, preferring to permit private trade that contributed to the growth of the economy. See Hong Lysa, *Siam in the Nineteenth Century: Evolution of Economy and Society* (Singapore: Institute of Southeast Asian Studies, 1984), Chapter 3.

[67] It is difficult to ascertain exactly what Si Suriyawong wanted to do. ร. ๕ รล-กห ๑๘/๒๐ refers to Si Suriyawong being sent to the South to "arrange matters." Specific problems mentioned are a rebellion by Chinese miners on Phuket, and *suai* and tin taxes. He was also to examine

The South had an unusually high concentration of Chinese workers employed in mining and other export enterprises. As noted above, these Chinese were integrated into the system in a different way than Siamese *phrai*. As hired workers, they proved more reliable as miners and plantation workers than *phrai* performing corvée.

There was also an unusually high concentration of tax farms in the South, again because of the prominence of industry there. Many of these tax farmers were also Chinese, and some were exceptionally powerful. The ultimate development in awarding authority to tax farmers was in Ranong, where the entire *meuang* was under what Damrong referred to as "chartered provincial administration." The local tin tax farmer assumed all judicial and official functions in exchange for collecting (and keeping) all taxes and running a private import-export company.[68] Hong maintains that this arrangement did not lead to the abuse of power because the tax farmers could not afford to drive away their labor supply.[69]

Perhaps because of the strength of the tax farming system in the South, Bangkok seems to have had more power to control appointments there, but ironically seems to have had less control over the *meuang* once those appointments were made.[70] There were good strategic reasons for wanting the *meuang* of the South to be more powerful than those of the North and Northeast. Transportation and movement of troops along the peninsula were difficult and slow. If the South were attacked by Burma, it would be difficult for Bangkok to respond quickly; strong *meuang* were needed for defense. Conversely, the difficulty of moving troops meant that strong *meuang* in the South were unlikely to pose a threat to Bangkok in the case of rebellion.[71]

---

the manpower rolls. Damrong's report, ม ๒.๑๔/๗๔, says that Si Suriyawong rearranged the administration in a decimal fashion, with "*nai* of tens," "*nai* of hundreds" and so on. He says that this was not successful because the administration "fell back into its old ways, which they all knew from generations back." See especially p. 47. In the North, too, early reforms were ignored by the local officials as soon as the commissioner left town. See ร. ๕ ม ๕๔/๓๓.

[68] Damrong, "Chartered Provincial Administration," translated in *Political Economy of Siam 1851-1910*, ed. Chatthip Nartsupha and Suthy Prasartset (Bangkok: Social Science Association of Thailand, 1978), pp. 419-20. This arrangement was intended to increase investment in tin mining by providing security to the investors. See especially pp. 421-2. For a detailed account of the Chinese family that governed Ranong, see Jennifer Cushman, *Family and State: The Formation of a Sino-Thai Tin-Mining Dynasty, 1797-1932* (New York: Oxford University Press, 1991).

[69] Hong, "Tax-Farming System," p. 390.

[70] Ian Brown, *The Elite and the Economy in Siam, c. 1890-1920* (Singapore: Oxford University Press, 1988), pp. 103-4; and Constance Wilson, "State and Society in the Reign of King Mongkut, 1851-1868: Thailand on the eve of Modernization" (PhD Dissertation, Cornell University, 1970), p. 125. Both comment on Bangkok's loose control in the South. In the Third Reign the *cao meuang* of Nakhon Si Thammarat had the power to negotiate treaties with the English, and all his sons got major administrative positions in other *meuang* in the South. Yet one son, the *cao meuang* of Phathalung, was denied promotion to *cao* of Nakhon Si Thammarat on his father's death, and was instead transferred to Bangkok. See อริยา, "เจ้าเมืองนครศรีธรรมราช" [Ariya, "The Governorship of Ligor"], pp. 104, 108.

[71] Wilson, "State and Society," p. 125.

The largest *meuang* of the South–Phathalung, Songkhla, and Nakhon Si Thammarat–shared the central Thai administrative scheme. Many of the smaller towns on the northern end of the peninsula shared some characteristics of this scheme as well and were much like *meuang* on the Central Plains. Farther to the south, however, more Malay characteristics and Malay titles appear. The Malay tributary states such as Kedah and Tregganu had entirely Malay administrations.

The relationship between the tributary states and Bangkok was not as different from the relationship between Bangkok and the major administrative centers as many authors have implied. In practice the distinction between tributaries and large, important *meuang* was blurred.[72] Just as a major *meuang* like Nakhon Si Thammarat sent silver and gold trees of tribute to Bangkok,[73] so did tributary states like Chiang Mai respond to instructions from the capital. Rama III actually drafted members of the retinue of *Cao* Anu of Vientiane–including Anu's son–to perform corvée when they came to Bangkok to attend the funeral of Rama II.[74] Bangkok approved appointments in the tributary states just as in the *meuang*.[75]

The primary difference between the tributaries and the other *meuang* was that the former did not have to pay regular tax assessments, but only periodic tribute. Otherwise, they were treated like very distant, very powerful *meuang*.[76]

THE CAPITAL AND THE COURT

Bangkok was in many ways like other *meuang*. It had its own *phrai* with their *nai*, and it had its own local officials. These individuals farmed and carried out their administrative tasks in much the same way as elsewhere. Bangkok was distinguished, however, by the presence of the supreme *cao* of *Meuang Thai*, the king.[77] Along with the king and his predominant authority came the court, the *suai* resources and corvée labor of other towns, and the largest population in the kingdom. These things constituted and conveyed the power of the king and that of the capital, the two being somewhat different things.

---

[72] See for instance Gesick, "Kingship and Political Integration," p. 150.

[73] The term used to describe the offering of tribute was the same in both cases—*banyakan* (which for some reason has been known in the literature by the Malay term *bunda mas*, despite the fact that the custom was practiced at least as far north as Chiang Rai). See for example ร. ๔ รล-กห ๒๙/๑๕๑ and ๗๐/๑๕๐ for Nakhon Si Thammarat.

[74] David Wyatt, "Siam and Laos, 1767-1827," *Journal of Southeast Asian History* 4,2 (1963): 29. This incident is dealt with in detail in Mayoury and Pheuiphanh, *Paths to Conflagration*, pp. 142-4.

[75] Rama IV, quoted in Rujaya, "Ratburi," p. 45. For examples see จดหมายเหตุ ร. ๔ ๑๒๑๔/๒๓, ๑๒๒๐/๑๗ and ๑๔.

[76] Wilson argues that Bangkok was actually more successful at exercising its authority in the tributary states than in the more formally subordinate *meuang*. Wilson, "State and Society," p. 520.

[77] One of the king's titles is *cao yu hua*, "the *cao* who is at the head."

The Advantages of the Capital

Bangkok's chief resource was its population, roughly twenty to thirty times greater than that of the next largest population center.[78] This population was supported by the unsurpassed suitability of the area for wet-rice cultivation. On the southern Caophraya flood plain, in the immediate area of Bangkok, " . . . live the largest concentrations of people who produce more than half the rice of Thailand on slightly less than half of the lands devoted to rice production."[79] In a political system where the control of people constitutes power, and in an environment where the most efficient transportation is by boat, having the majority of the population living on an abundant food source next to a river presented multiple advantages.

The location of the capital had other advantages. Situated near the mouth of the river that drains most of Thailand north of the Malay peninsula, this is a natural location for a port. It is accessible by boat from the sea and by river from the interior. This gave the ruler of Bangkok an important advantage in trade, the profits from which could be considerable. Many of the goods that came into Bangkok as *suai* tax payments were channeled into trade.

Contrary to the claim by some Europeans that Siam existed in Japanese-style isolation until the Bowring Treaty of the Fourth Reign,[80] an important part of the king's income traditionally came from trade with China. Most of this trade was carried in Chinese ships, and it was treated as local trade in China, although Siamese had invested heavily in the cargoes. This trade was an important source of income for the nobility, but the king also had a special resource in the form of royal tribute missions.[81] These missions were granted trading privileges and tax exemptions in China. The Siamese were extremely enthusiastic about these missions because they generated large profits. Although they were expected to send missions triennially, Rama I came up with excuses to send twenty-two tribute missions to China in his twenty-seven year reign. It was usual to send more than the stipulated three ships per mission as well.[82] The Chinese tolerated such behavior for many years, partly because they expected such things from "barbarians," but mostly because they needed Siamese rice to offset chronic shortages in south China.[83] Eventually it became too much even for the tribute-greedy Chinese, who in 1839 reduced the

---

[78] The next largest center was the old capital, Ayuthaya. Sternstein estimates that Bangkok's population in the mid-nineteenth century was 300,000, and he argues that the central government's policy towards the smaller *meuang* was deliberately designed to keep the control of the population divided, so that there was no rival concentration of manpower anywhere else. See Sternstein, "Thai Centres," p. 71.

[79] Lucien Hanks, *Rice and Man: Agricultural Ecology in Southeast Asia* (Chicago: Aldive-Atherton, 1972), p. 7.

[80] See for instance Holt Hallett, *A Thousand Miles On An Elephant in the Shan States* (London: William Blackwood & Sons, 1890), p. 116.

[81] Jennifer Cushman, *Fields from the Sea: Chinese Junk Trade with Siam During the Late Eighteenth and Early Nineteenth Centuries* (Ithaca: Cornell Southeast Asia Program Publications, 1993), Chapter 1.

[82] Sarasin Viraphol, *Tribute and Profit: Sino-Siamese Trade, 1652-1853* (Cambridge, MA: Harvard University Press, 1977), pp. 181, 155. In the Third Reign Crawfurd estimated the profits of this trade to average 300 percent. Ibid., p. 191.

[83] Ibid., Chapter 5. Import duties on rice were often reduced or waived. However, more profitable items such as pepper and sappanwood were carried in larger volumes than rice. See Cushman, *Fields from the Sea*, Chapter 4.

Siamese tribute requirement to one mission every four years. This decision had no particular impact on Thai policy.[84] When the frequency of tribute missions did decline, it did so rapidly. This happened as a result of the elimination of Siamese royal monopolies, due to treaty obligations; as a result of a reduction in the amount of *suai* goods available to the crown, due to the increasing popularity of commuting taxes in kind to cash; and as a result of internal turmoil in China, which made trade a much riskier proposition.[85]

A favorable trading location, natural abundance, and a comparatively dense population all made Bangkok an attractive spot for the capital. Once the capital was erected there, this in turn drew the court and nobles who further increased the town's power with their personal retinues and wealth, but also complicated the king's control over policy.

Noble Families

Powerful court families could be an impediment to the power of the king, but they increased the power of the capital vis-à-vis the other *meuang*. When the interests of the king and the court concurred, the capital could exercise unparalleled power over the other *meuang* of the kingdom. When they did not, the nobility could and did limit the power of the king.

The process of selecting kings illustrates the power of the nobility. Although all the kings of the Bangkok period have been of the same lineage, prior to the reign of King Chulalongkorn they were never able to settle the issue of their own succession. Kings were selected from the available princes of high rank by a council of senior ministers.

The composition of this council was fluid: " . . . no hard and fast rules exist as to how electors are qualified as such, but they were usually royal and temporal lords of the realm sometimes doing their business in the presence, but not with the participation, of spiritual lords."[86] Its composition was never formally fixed, but the council would necessarily include the most important government officials, that is those members of the court sufficiently powerful to create trouble for a new king whose selection they did not approve. The decision making was probably consensual, although the selections of Rama IV and V were clearly dominated by the Bunnag family. Rama III improved his chances by building alliances among officials, but even he needed Bunnag support to become king.

Any king so chosen would then be beholden to those who selected him. It was not royal gratitude alone that ensured this; the power of the ministers did, too. The ministers had personal connections and patron-client relationships with their subordinates that enabled them to subvert the king's will.

The accession of Rama III demonstrates that the succession was not determined strictly by birth. As a prince Rama III had been very active in the government, serving as a general against the Burmese and supervising the Phra Khlang, which

---

[84] Ibid., p. 194. The suggestion of the Chien Lung Emperor in 1790 that Siamese tribute missions should be reduced to one in ten years had no effect either.

[85] At the same time that the Chinese junk trade declined, unequal treaties negotiated between European countries and the Chinese after the Opium Wars made it more attractive to ship Siamese cargoes in European hulls. Cushman, *Fields from the Sea*, Chapter 7.

[86] Prince Dhani, "The Old Siamese Conception of the Monarchy," *Journal of the Siam Society* 36,2 (1947): 100.

had jurisdiction over the Ministry of Ports and of one of the main treasuries. According to Vella, " . . . it appeared to Europeans that [he] had taken over all important matters of state" by the death of Rama II.[87] He therefore had personal connections which made him a formidable contender for the throne, despite the fact that there were two princes superior to him in rank.

Despite the king's personal power, though, the Third Reign saw an increase in the influence of the Bunnag family. The Bunnags had been very prominent in the Ayuthaya government and had reasserted themselves after the reconquest of the kingdom and the deposition of King Taksin.[88] In the Third Reign Dit Bunnag managed to secure two of the most important ministries for himself, those of the Phra Khlang and the Kalahom, the Ministry of the South. He held these simultaneously, a feat unique in the Bangkok period. He then rapidly multiplied his connections in other ministries and in the Royal Pages corps, and by the death of Rama III he had attained the position of kingmaker. The newly crowned Rama IV rewarded him and his brother, giving them the highest possible noble rank, *somdet caophraya*, and "almost unlimited powers."[89]

Fortunately for the new Rama IV, the elder Bunnags had little time to exercise these powers; both died four years later. Their children kept up the family tradition, however: Dit's son Chuang became *Caophraya* Si Suriyawong, Minister of the Kalahom, and also a kingmaker. Through his personal power and family connections he was able to insure the selection of Chulalongkorn as king on the death of Rama IV. He too extracted his reward, becoming a *somdet caophraya* in his turn and also the regent to the underage Rama V. His brother Thuam became Phra Khlang, his son Wan became Kalahom, and he distributed various other relatives throughout the government. This gave him the power that King Chulalongkorn would later recall made the Regency period and his early reign so miserable for him.[90] Wyatt tells the following apocryphal story about Chuang:

> Oral tradition has it that one of the granddaughters of the last great Bunnag statesman, Chaophraya Si Suriyawong (Chuang), once asked him, "Grandfather, why don't you become King?" He is said to have replied, "Why should I bother? I have everything a man could desire."[91]

Nobles and officials of families less successful than the Bunnags were still a drain on the resources of the king, because they were eager to command their own network

---

[87] Vella, *Siam Under Rama III*, p. 11. Wyatt puts it more modestly: " . . . he had long played a leading, responsible role in government." See David Wyatt, *Thailand: A Short History* (New Haven: Yale University Press, 1982), p. 167.

[88] David Wyatt, "Family Politics in Nineteenth Century Thailand," *Journal of Southeast Asian History* 9,2 (1968): 212, 216-20.

[89] Ibid., p. 221.

[90] พระบาทสมเด็จพระจุลจอมเกล้า, "พระบรมราโชวาทถึงเจ้าฟ้ามหาวชิรุณหิศ" [King Chulalong-korn, "Letter to Prince Mahawachirunhit"], in ชัยอนันต์ สมุทวณิช และ ขัตติยา กรรณสูต รวบ-รวม, *เอกสารการเมืองการปกครองไทย (พศ ๒๔๑๗ - ๒๔๗๗)* [Chai-anan Samudavanija and Khatthiya Kansut, ed., *Thai Political and Administrative Documents (BE 2417 - 2477)*] (Bang-kok: Social Science Association of Thailand, BE 2532), p. 104.

[91] Wyatt, "Family Politics," p. 224.

of *phrai*. A good position at court meant that one was in a good position to be a patron as well. Thus we sometimes find that *phrai* and criminals fled not to the forest, but to the capital.[92] King Mongkut had to issue decrees forbidding officials and princes from claiming the *phrai* or slaves of other masters. When this happens, he wrote, " . . . the *cao mu, munnai* and creditors cannot contact [their *phrai* or slaves], fearing the merit of the house or palace."[93] Early in the Fifth Reign the head of the Department of the Registrar (*Krom* Phrasurasawadi) complained that the government collected only about a third of the taxes due from *phrai* officially registered to the palace itself.[94]

While the noble families could resist the power of the king, their considerable resources contributed to the power of the capital. As a result of this concentration of resources Bangkok dominated a remarkably large area, given the technological conditions and terrain involved. However, the capital could exercise its considerable power only when the court and the king concurred. Where their interests diverged they limited each other's power. The situation was so bad during the Fourth Reign that Rama IV actually issued a proclamation reminding officials to obey his proclamations.[95] Tej Bunnag reports that in an 1891 cabinet meeting the king complained that he only effectively controlled the *meuang* of Nonthaburi, Prathum Thani, Phrapradaeng, and Samut Prakan.[96] This is because officials of the court firmly controlled the other Inner provinces.

When the interests of both the king and the court were challenged, they could muster a formidable response. Thus, Taksin and Rama I were able to reconquer the entire kingdom that had been Ayuthaya. When *Cao* Anu rebelled and threatened Bangkok itself, Rama III was able to overwhelm his forces and raze Vientiane to the ground.[97] Rama III and IV conducted lengthy campaigns to depopulate the east bank of the Mekong, an enterprise that consumed considerable resources at the farthest edges of the kingdom and forced large-scale migrations.[98] The ill-fated Chiang Tung

[92] E.g. ร. ๕ ม ๒.๑๒ก แผนกปกครอง (ใบบอก) นครราชสีมา ล. ๑ ปีกที้ ๕.

[93] ประภาส, *ประชุมประกาศ ร. ๔*[Praphat, *Collected Proclamations of the Fourth Reign*] vol. 1, #140, p. 263. Proclamation # 161, pp. 305-6, indicates a similar problem with escaped prisoners seeking the protection of powerful houses.

[94] ร. ๕ บ ๑๗/๔๑.

[95] "ประกาศให้ผู้รับพระบรมราชโองการฟังรับสั่งให้ชัดเจน" ["Proclamation That Those Receiving Royal Decrees Listen to Them Clearly"], in ประภาส, *ประชุมประกาศ ร. ๔* [Praphat, *Collected Proclamations of the Fourth Reign*] vol. 1, #175, p. 332.

[96] Tej, *Provincial Administration*, p. 19. These are the towns closest to Bangkok, and two of the four have now been absorbed into the Bangkok metropolitan area.

[97] Mayoury and Pheuiphanh, *Paths to Conflagration*, Chapters 7 and 8 give a detailed, if somewhat biased, account of this campaign. What emerges most clearly is the lopsided nature of the contest, the Siamese armies easily defeating the smaller, poorly equipped Lao forces. As a partial corrective to their account, see Wilson, "State and Society," pp. 127-8.

[98] Breazeale, "Integration of the Lao States," Chapter 1, and Snit and Breazeale, *Phuan*, pp. 17-34, 53-5. The migrations from the east bank presumably made it possible to reward those officials whose resources were called upon to mount the campaign.

expeditions involved mobilizing considerable forces in some of the roughest terrain in Southeast Asia.[99]

The essential problem confronting kings who wished to initiate reform, therefore, was to exert control over the central government. If this could be accomplished, and more responsive ministers put in place, then the king gained formidable power resources to match his traditional authority. This was the pattern followed by King Chulalongkorn. He first asserted control over the central government—in his case, by waiting until powerful figures left over from earlier reigns died off and then by replacing them with loyal followers of his own. Only then did he begin provincial reform.

THE ADMINISTRATIVE STRUCTURE OF THE CAPITAL

The basic administrative structure of the capital was much like that of the *meuang* of the Central Plains and the larger regional *meuang*. Ministries and other large manpower units, called *krom*, were under the control of princes and important officials. These were subdivided into smaller *krom* and *kaung*, each with its own *nai*.[100]

The most important characteristic distinguishing Bangkok from the other *meuang* was the presence of large *krom* responsible for provincial affairs, which meant that they were responsible for subordinate *meuang*. The two most powerful of these ministries were the Mahathai and the Kalahom, which had jurisdiction over the *meuang* of the North and the South respectively. At the end of the Ayuthaya period the Kalahom had fallen into disfavor. Rather than replace the minister, the *meuang* under the control of the Kalahom were simply transferred to *Krom* Tha, the Department of the Port. Rama I transferred most of the southern *meuang* back to the Kalahom, but *Krom* Tha retained its authority over some of the coastal *meuang* closest to Bangkok.[101] Thus, in the early Bangkok period there were three ministries with provincial responsibilities: the Mahathai, the Kalahom, and *Krom* Tha.

Ostensibly each of these ministries once had specialized functions. The Mahathai was supposed to have handled "civilian affairs," primarily taxation and justice. The Kalahom was supposed to have been responsible for military affairs. *Krom* Tha was supposed to have been responsible for trade duties and tariffs. These functions were supposed to have been exercised by the respective ministries throughout the entire kingdom.[102] If it was ever so, these ministries rapidly lost such specialized functions,

---

[99] See พระเจ้าน้องยาเธอ กรมหมื่น ไชนาทเรนทร รวบรวม, จดหมายเหตุเรื่องทัพเชียงตุง [Prince Chainatrenthon, ed., *Documents on the Soldiers of Chiang Tung*] (Bangkok: Memorial Volume for Admiral Phraya Nawaphol Phayurak, BE 2459).

[100] On *krom* and *kaung* in the capital, see Wilson, "State and Society," pp. 326-43.

[101] พระบาทสมเด็จพระจุลจอมเกล้าเจ้าอยู่หัว, "พระราชาธิบายแก้ไขการปกครอง" [King Chulalong-korn, "Royal Explanation of the Improvements in the Administration"], in ชัยอนันต์ และ ขัตติ-ยา รวบรวม, เอกสาร [Chai-anan and Khatthiya, eds., *Documents*], p. 73.

[102] Ibid., pp. 72-3. This heretofore mythical specialization of functions was revived in the Fifth Reign, when these duties were "reassigned" to the ministries which had supposedly originally performed them. This revival of old government structures illustrates the essentially conservative nature of the radical reforms of the Fifth Reign.

and thereafter each exercised complete authority, but only over its assigned *meuang*.[103]

Below the level of the territorial ministries, there were four other ministries of less prestige. Called the "Four Pillars," they retained specialized functions, but were largely confined to the business of running the court and the capital. The first, the Department of the Palace [*Krom* Wang], ran the daily affairs of the palace and coordinated the royal rituals.

The second, the Department of the City [*Krom* Meuang], conducted the daily affairs of the capital and assisted with tax collection and recruiting corvée laborers. In many respects the head of this *krom*, Caophraya Yommarat, was much like the *cao meuang* of other towns. He and his officials were responsible for corvée and tax collection, and in time of war he might be asked to raise and lead troops like any other *cao meuang*.[104]

The third was the Department of the Treasury [*Krom* Khlang]. This *krom* received taxes and disbursed funds. In fact responsibility for collecting taxes became dispersed among a number of competing treasuries in other *krom*. Wilson counts no less than eighteen treasuries receiving income from tax farms alone in the Fourth Reign.[105] The Department of the Treasury then came to resemble a privy purse, handling the funds most directly accessible to the king.

The fourth of the Four Pillars, the Department of the Fields [*Krom* Na], was the only one to have much contact with the *meuang*. This is because it was responsible for collecting the rice field tax. In theory this was an annual tax on the produce of all *meuang*. In practice it was collected with varying regularity.[106] A royal commissioner would be sent out to conduct a survey of the local rice fields to estimate production. Not knowing the area, he would have to rely on local officials to show him around. These officials were admonished to be honest and thorough. The royal commissioner would make up a series of tickets indicating how much tax each farmer owed, and these tickets were then forwarded to the local officials. The local officials, in turn, would remit the tax to the royal commissioners, and the tickets would become both tax receipts and the closest thing to a title deed that existed under the old system.[107] Even here, where we have a case of a functionally specialized department interacting

---

[103] The *Krom* Tha did retain some specialized authority over trade conducted at Bangkok, and it also functioned as a kind of Ministry of Foreign Affairs, because its officials had experience dealing with foreign traders.

[104] See for instance ไชยนาทเรนทร รวบรวม, *เรื่องทัพเชียงตุง* [Chainatrenthon, ed., *Soldiers of Chiang Tung*].

[105] Wilson, "State and Society," p. 632.

[106] One town in the Northeast—Phicit—was discovered to have never paid the rice tax. คมเนตร, "อำนาจท้องถิ่นแบบจารีต" [Khomnet, "Traditional Local Power"], p. 37.

[107] ร. ๔ รล-กห ๑๑/๔๔ is an example of the instructions given to the Royal commissioner and local officials. The records for rice field tax collection in the South seem to be more complete than for other parts of the kingdom, but it is not clear that this means that the tax was collected there more regularly, or if the records for other parts of the kingdom were lost. จดหมายเหตุ ร. ๔ ๑๒๐๗/๔๔ simply orders a flat increase in rice tax from Nakhon Ratchasima, perhaps indicating that the formality of surveying the *meuang* was sometimes dispensed with. Even today tax receipts are sometimes used as proof of land rights in Thailand.

closely with the *meuang* and sending out inspectors, we also see the dependence of the central government on local officials for critical information.

Beneath the level of the Four Pillars were a confusing mass of *krom*, some assigned to royalty as their personal retinue, some to officials, some ostensibly functional, some actually providing specialized services. Some of these were permanent, while others were dissolved upon the death of the *nai* and their manpower redistributed.[108]

The king seems to have been able to redistribute manpower between departments in the capital at will, so long as he had the information necessary to locate people. There were constraints on moving manpower out of other *meuang*, though. For instance, King Chulalongkorn created a Department of Telegraphs to handle telegraph construction. Attempts to transfer *phrai* from *meuang* Lopburi to this *krom* met with a storm of local protest. From then on, he instead created a separate Department of Telegraphs within each town so that the *phrai* would still be formally part of their old *meuang*.[109]

One *krom* that deserves particular mention is the Department of the Registrar [*Krom* Phrasurasawadi]. This was the *krom* charged with keeping the manpower rolls for the entire kingdom. Its function corresponded to that of parallel institutions in the *meuang*, called *krom satsadi*.

Krom Phrasurasawadi was the linchpin of the old system. Its records made possible the collection of *suai* and the recruitment of corvée. It also handled the tattooing of *phrai* in the capital and nearby provinces. Whenever new rolls were completed in any of the *meuang*, officials of the local *krom satsadi* were supposed to send copies to *krom* Phrasurasawadi. The great tattooing expeditions to the *meuang* were designed to improve the records available to *Krom* Phrasurasawadi.

Because of its importance, great care was taken in the selection of the head of *Krom* Phrasurasawadi. Only close supporters of the king were appointed to the position.[110] However, no matter how much care was taken in selecting this official, the *krom* still faced all the problems of the old manpower system, and it was never able perfectly to track the kingdom's manpower.[111]

All of the problems of the old manpower system were distilled in *Krom* Phrasurasawadi. Although the *krom* could send out officials to check up on *nai*, they were dependent on the cooperation of local officials to get anything done. *Nai* were often lax about bringing in their *phrai* to be registered, and they connived with *phrai* to hide them from central government officials. Thus the rolls were never really accurate. Local patrons were prompt, however, about requesting tax reductions for *phrai* who were crippled, old, dead, or absent because they had fled. Early in the Fifth Reign the head of the *krom* complained to the king that "nowadays the [number of] people who render royal service of all kinds are reduced monthly by the chiefs of their groups subtracting them; we cannot hope to have enough to use."[112]

---

[108] See Wilson, "State and Society," pp. 336-43.

[109] ร. ๕ รล-พศ ๓๑, pp. 82-6.

[110] อัญชลี, "ระบบไพร่" [Anchalee, "Phrai System"], p. 245.

[111] ปิยะฉัตร, ระบบไพร่ [Piyachat, *Phrai System*], p. 99.

[112] ร. ๕ รล-พศ ๓/๑๓๑, pp. 142-3; see also รล-พศ ๗ ที่ ๔๐, pp. 59-60.

The Uparat

The king also faced rivals within the royal family. In the intensely personalistic Siamese political system, where loyalty was accorded to the official rather than to the office, frustrated pretenders to the throne were potentially a very serious problem for a king. The practice therefore developed of trying to co-opt the king's most powerful rival by granting him the position of *uparat*, sometimes referred to as a "vice-king." The *uparat* occupied the Front Palace and had an administration of his own, parallel to that of the Grand Palace. This included an army, considerable tax revenue, and substantial numbers of *phrai*, both in the capital and in the *meuang* of the Central Plains. In theory at least this arrangement co-opted the second most powerful person in the kingdom, bringing him into the official hierarchy.

While the *uparat* may have brought more people into the system through alternative patronage networks, the office obviously posed certain problems from the perspective of developing a coherent royal policy, and it tended to become a focal point for discontent.[113] Even in the relatively harmonious relationship between Rama IV and his *uparat*, Phraphinklao, there was considerable tension.[114] Poor relations between a king and his *uparat* could lead to virtual civil war, as happened early in the Fifth Reign. No king of the Bangkok period ever replaced an *uparat* who predeceased him.

A Note on the "Galactic Polity"

Tambiah has emphasized the replication of the institutions of the central government at the local level in the "galactic polities" of Southeast Asia, as has Clifford Geertz in *Negara* and Ronald Inden in his idea of "a scale of forms" in *Imagining India*.[115] These authors have all concentrated on the geographical layout of the capital as a replication of the cosmological structure of the universe, in which localities become satellites that seek in turn to replicate the capital.[116]

While this is all true at the level of cosmology, it focuses on aesthetics and obscures the more practical point that local centers had to perform many of the same administrative tasks as the capital. Unlike governments in modern states, there was relatively little division of labor between the capital and local centers. The capital was in a sense simply the first among equals, and one could equally well say that the capital emulated the localities in its administrative practice.

It is not clear how much cosmological replication really went on. In Siam there was a good deal of regional variation, both in administrative practice and in symbolic matters such as the naming of offices. In the South local officials were referred to by the Malay term *Tonku*, for instance. In the Northeast the administrative model of Lan Chang was followed, rather than that of Bangkok. Neither of these variations was

---

[113] ณัฐวุฒิ สุทธิสงคราม, *สมเด็จเจ้าพระยาบรมมหาศรีสุริยวงส์* [Natthawutthi Sutthisongkram, *Somdet Caophraya Borommaha Si Suriyawong*], vol. 1 (Bangkok: Si Tham, BE 2404), pp. 815-25, argues that there was a long tradition of conflict between kings and their *uparat*.

[114] Wyatt, *Short History*, p. 182.

[115] See Clifford Geertz, *Negara: The Theatre State in Nineteenth-Century Bali* (Princeton: Princeton University Press, 1980); and Ronald Inden, *Imagining India* (New York: Blackwell, 1990).

[116] On the Thai capital, see A. Thomas Kirsch, "Modernizing Implications of Nineteenth-Century Reforms in the Thai Sangha," in *Religion and Legitimation of Power in Thailand, Laos, and Burma*, ed. Bardwell Smith (Chambersburg, PA: Anima, 1978), pp. 55-6.

perceived by Bangkok as a symbolic assertion of independence or as a challenge to its authority.

The point is important because the "galactic polity" approach privileges court ideology over local politics. It accepts that the cultural products of the court accurately represent how people ordinarily thought about their political relationships. Yet as we have seen, the court's official political theory had only tenuous links with the practice of politics at any level. Court nobles did not respect the king's will simply because he occupied the throne and conducted the proper rituals—they defied him often, and often got away with it. Similarly, *phrai* did not obey simply because a *nai* was superior to them. They often fled or made alternative connections with patrons that enabled them to defy their *nai* and evade their responsibilities.

Different kings had different attitudes toward royal rituals, but modernizers like Rama IV and Rama V felt free to modify and simplify them.[117] Nor did the officials of the *meuang* obey instructions from the capital because of the cosmological significance of its construction. Even the most cursory glance at the layout of Ratanakosin Island shows that it lacks the sophisticated symmetry required to fulfill its role as the center of the cosmos; the same was true of Ayuthaya before it.

There was certainly a cultural dimension to the conduct of politics in the old system. But that culture did not operate at the level of structural-functional patterns or idealized aggregate behavior; it operated at the level of individual actions and choices made by people trying to maneuver through life in the best way they knew how. To the degree that patterns exist, they were the product of people acting in the ways that seemed best to them. The obedience or disobedience of nobles, officials, *nai, phrai*, and slaves were all the product of strategies and choices made by people, not cultural paragons. These strategies and choices were informed by culture. Individuals learned from others what goals were worth pursuing and how to go about attaining them, so that both reasons for obeying and techniques for cheating were embodied in Siamese political culture. To isolate one strand artificially—to focus on the construction of the capital, say, or the official ideology promulgated by the court—gives us an impoverished and stilted view of a rich civilization, which was actually full of people with conflicting interests, multiple goals, and a need to cooperate, all creatively engaged in trying to improve their lives.

The political institutions of the kingdom were well adapted for keeping *phrai* in the system, but the cost from the perspective of the throne was that much of the control over day-to-day affairs was devolved to the local level. Kings had both the authority to control activity at the local level and the ambition to centralize power. These were constrained by the realities of trying to control people who were widely scattered throughout a difficult and sparsely populated terrain, people who had schemata for political life that emphasized personal authority over institutional rules. Kings tried to reform the system in ways that would give them greater power and more direct authority over people at the grassroots level, but as long as they operated within the logic of the old system they were forced to tolerate the devolution of power, in their own interest. King Chulalongkorn was able to centralize power only

---

[117] See H. G. Quaritch Wales, *Siamese State Ceremonies: Their History and Function* (London: Bernard Quaritch, 1931), especially Chapter 4.

after exposure to a fully developed alternative set of schemata, developed in another culture, that provided a solution to this traditional problem.

Chapter 5

CONCEPTUAL CHANGE AND INSTITUTIONAL INNOVATION

The ideal type of early Bangkok period Siamese government constructed above emphasizes the logic of the old system, beginning with the schemata used to understand political life, and then demonstrating how self-interest generated behavior and institutions very different from those found in modern states. This synchronic approach may give the impression that the system was static. However, it actually changed over time to accommodate variation in the international and local environment. Change came in the form of both cross-cultural borrowing of schemata and indigenous innovations. Below I sketch some of the more important changes over time, emphasizing the Fifth Reign reforms that eventually destroyed the old system and created the foundations of the modern Thai state. The timing and content of these reforms were strongly influenced by the cultural conditions sketched above, as much as by the European models they adapted.

The first two reigns of the Bangkok period were primarily devoted to reconstructing the kingdom. The primary problem for Rama I and II was securing the loyalty of important regional leaders and insuring the kingdom's security against attack from outside. Both goals required ongoing military campaigns, and thus martial endeavors took precedence over institutional innovation during these reigns.

Already in this period there were indications of tax evasion and concealment of *phrai*, as discussed above. These were endemic problems that perpetually plagued the system. After these first two reigns kings began to experiment with innovative political ideas, as the long-term trends which would ultimately undermine the system and lead to its destruction began to manifest themselves; these included economic change, contact with the West, extraterritoriality, and missionary protégés. Thus, I begin with a brief sketch of the reign of Rama III.

THE THIRD REIGN (1824-1851)

Following the reconstitution of the kingdom by Rama I and II, the Third Reign saw two major initiatives designed to increase the resources available to the throne: the development of tax farming, and the extension of tattooing to the Northeast. Vella argues that budgetary shortfalls in the Second Reign and increased spending in the Third led Rama III to seek out new resources.[1] A number of factors contributed to this development, among them the declining value of the tributary trade with China,

---

[1] Walter Vella, *Siam Under Rama III, 1824-1851* (Locust Valley, NY: J. J. Augustin, 1957), p. 19.

losses sustained in trade by Rama II, restrictions on royal monopolies agreed to in the Burney Treaty of 1826, increasing commutation of *suai* obligations to cash payments, and increasing royal expenditures.

Tax farming dramatically increased in scope in the Third Reign. King Mongkut (Rama IV) believed that his predecessor was influenced by the Chinese example in deciding to expand tax farming because he equated it with more advanced civilizations.[2] However, Rama IV was probably also attuned to the political advantages of having local revenue collectors depend on royal pleasure to retain their positions.[3]

As Hong has pointed out, the shift to tax farming was made feasible by the internal growth of the Siamese economy. Tax farms had existed in Siam since the Ayuthaya period, but in the First and Second Reigns of the Bangkok period the economic situation had been so chaotic, and trade so disrupted, that tax farming was largely impractical and would have had deleterious effects on the kingdom's recovery from the Burmese invasion and subsequent civil wars.[4]

The process of consolidating the kingdom begun in the first two reigns continued in the Third. The enforcement of corvée service and *suai* collection may have increased in the Third Reign. B. J. Terwiel, for instance, argues that the Siamese government was becoming more oppressive in the Central Plains in the first half of the nineteenth century, meaning by this that it was extracting more resources. His evidence is highly indirect, though.[5]

One dimension of this consolidation involved increasing Bangkok's control over the Northeast. The tattooing of *phrai* was introduced into the region in the late 1820s.[6] This increased Siamese control over the region and enabled the central government to mobilize more resources from the Northeast. It also reflected the symbolic reduction of the Lao *meuang* from quasi-independent political entities to full-fledged members of the Siamese kingdom. This formal subordination bred unrest among the Lao of the region. Mayoury and Pheuiphanh argue that the extension of tattooing to

---

[2] Hong Lysa, "The Tax-Farming System in the Early Bangkok Period," *Journal of Southeast Asian Studies* 14,2 (1983): 384-5.

[3] Ibid., pp. 383-5. See also Sarasin Viraphol, *Tribute and Profit: Sino-Siamese Trade, 1652-1853* (Cambridge, MA: Harvard University Press, 1977), p. 223; Vella, *Rama III*, p. 23; and Sompop Manarungsan, *Economic Development of Thailand, 1850-1950: Response to the Challenge of the World Economy* (Bangkok: Chulalongkorn University, Institute of Asian Studies, 1989), pp. 10-11. As noted above, tax farmers were initially seen as competitors or intruders by the *caos*, but later these groups learned to accommodate each other. The revenues from tax farming were on the decline by the Fifth Reign, however. This was in part because of the rigging of the auctions by Chinese secret societies, and in part because of princes who extended tax-exemptions to their clients. See Hong, "The Tax-Farming System," pp. 395-6.

[4] Ibid., p. 384.

[5] As it would have to be, given the incomplete state of the tax records from the period. He cites the increase in alcoholism and gambling as evidence of a declining quality of life, although they could also be due to promotion of these activities by the alcohol and gambling tax farmers. B. J. Terwiel, *Through Travellers' Eyes: An Approach to Nineteenth-Century Thai History* (Bangkok: Duang Komol, 1989), p. 251.

[6] Junko Koizumi, "Commutation of *Suai* from Northeast Thailand in the Middle of the Nineteenth Century," *Journal of Southeast Asian Studies* 23,2 (1992): 279-81.

the Northeast was one of the factors that precipitated the revolt of *Cao* Anu of Vientiane in 1827.[7]

The *Cao* Anu revolt ended disastrously for Vientiane, and large numbers of Lao from the left bank of the Mekong were compelled to migrate west, into areas more securely within Bangkok's reach. About forty new *meuang* were created in the Northeast,[8] and additional people were resettled near Bangkok. Tax collection was increased.

Bangkok also increased its control over the South during the Third Reign, following rebellions in Saiburi (Kedah), Kelantan, and Pattani. As discussed above, the Siamese under Rama II had attempted to supplant the Malay sultans of the *meuang* with appointees from Bangkok. Periodic rebellions ensued, until Rama III reinstated the sultans, who then helped stabilize the area under Siamese suzerainty. Bangkok's control over the region was thus actually improved by delegating authority to local notables, rather than by trying to impose its own governors, a dramatic example of the logic of the old system in action.

Rama III's efforts to increase the power and resources of the capital followed traditional strategies. He increased revenues by expanding the existing tax farming system. He increased the number of *phrai* in the formal hierarchy of the kingdom by extending tattooing to the Northeast and by resettling war captives close to the capital. War was used as a tool to increase population growth.

However, even as Rama III pursued these traditional strategies, the international environment was changing. The British fought a war with Burma during the Third Reign, annexing part of that kingdom in 1826. This caused concern in Bangkok that the British might ultimately develop designs on Siam as well. It also increased British interest in Siam, now a neighbor. In 1826 Siam and Britain signed the Burney Treaty, characterized by Wyatt as providing Siam with a measure of security in exchange for commercial concessions.[9] The treaty stimulated trade and contact with Europeans and promoted an increased familiarity with Western culture and ideas, familiarity which would have important political consequences in the Fourth and Fifth Reigns.

THE FOURTH REIGN (1851-1868)

The Fourth Reign was characterized by enormous changes in Siam's foreign relations, which in turn set off ripple effects in the Kingdom's domestic politics and economy. A growing export market in rice, in particular, accelerated changes in the economy and undermined the traditional political system.

At the same time, increased contact with the West exposed some Siamese to European culture. By making new schemata available to key political actors, including the heir to the throne, this cross-cultural contact laid the foundations for future changes in Siamese political culture.

---

[7] Mayoury Ngaosyvathn and Pheuiphanh Ngaosyvathn, *Paths to Conflagration: Fifty Years of Diplomacy and Warfare in Laos, Thailand, and Vietnam, 1778-1828* (Ithaca: Cornell Southeast Asia Program, 1998), pp. 144-8. On their own evidence, however, it appears that Anu himself instituted reforms along the lines of the Siamese model in order to increase his own access to the Lao kingdom's resources. Ibid., pp. 88-90.

[8] David Wyatt, *Thailand: A Short History* (New Haven: Yale University Press, 1982), p. 171.

[9] Ibid., p. 169.

Foreign Relations and Domestic Repercussions

Because of internal turmoil in China following the Opium War and the Taiping rebellion, the value and quantity of the China trade declined steadily in the mid-nineteenth century. On his accession to the throne Rama IV sent the traditional mission to request investiture. The first was turned back because of the recent death of the Emperor Tao-kuang. A second mission the following year was attacked and robbed by Taiping rebels on its return from Beijing. Rama IV declined to send any further missions.[10]

At the same time, treaty concessions won by Western countries following the Opium Wars made it more attractive to carry Siamese cargoes in European or American ships.[11] This meant the end of the royal privileges extended to Chinese merchants, which had done much to sustain the trade. The Fourth Reign thus saw the end of the old system of Chinese trade sponsored by Siamese nobles and royalty, and the creation of a new, Western-oriented system based on the Bowring Treaty.

Western, especially British, merchants were determined to conduct trade in Siam according to their own liberal principles. Furthermore, Rama IV had considerable contact with Europeans before ascending the throne and seems to have come to share some Liberal economic ideas. Even prior to the Bowring Treaty of 1855 he had unilaterally reduced import duties, allowed the export of rice, and abolished some royal monopolies.[12] The Bowring Treaty further opened up Siam to foreign trade.

The Bowring Treaty also granted extraterritorial jurisdiction to European consuls, gave foreigners rights to own property and reside in Bangkok, to travel and trade freely everywhere in the kingdom, and fixed import and export duties. By 1870 twelve European countries had virtually identical treaties with Siam.

Bowring was quite aware of the implications of the treaty:

> It was clear that my success involved a total change in the whole system of taxation—that it took a large proportion of the existing sources of revenue—that it uprooted a great number of privileges and monopolies which had not only long been established, but which were held by the most influential nobles and highest functionaries in the state.[13]

This was a significant blow to the old Siamese political system. The Bowring Treaty eroded the foundations of the old system in three ways.

First, it made the export of rice easier and attracted more European shipping, which increased the volume of exports. Precise figures are not available, but Ingram

---

[10] Sarasin, *Tribute and Profit*, pp. 232, 236. Chinese suzerainty and tribute obligations were only formally renounced by King Chulalongkorn in RS 101 (1882). Ibid., p. 237.

[11] Jennifer Cushman, *Fields from the Sea: Chinese Junk Trade with Siam During the Late Eighteenth and Early Nineteenth Centuries* (Ithaca: Cornell Southeast Asia Program Publications, 1993), pp. 135-6.

[12] James C. Ingram, *Economic Change in Thailand, 1850-1970* (Stanford: Stanford University Press, 1971), p. 33.

[13] Sir John Bowring, *The Kingdom and People of Siam*, vol. II (New York: Oxford University Press, 1967 [1857]), p. 226. These nobles and functionaries included the *Uparat* and the Phra Khlang. See especially p. 227. The Phra Khlang took the lead in supporting the treaty, however, apparently either because he was convinced concessions were necessary to placate the British, or because he had found a way to profit from the situation. Government revenues dropped only briefly after the treaty came into effect. Wyatt, *Short History*, p. 184.

estimates that in 1850 about 5 percent of Siam's total rice production was exported. In RS 126 (1907/8), the first year for which official figures are available, 51 percent of the harvest was exported.[14] Sompop argues the increase was slightly less, beginning at 5 percent for the period 1857-60, increasing to 25 percent by 1900, and 37 percent for 1906-10.[15] This increase was entirely through the initiative of what we would call the private sector.

Increasing rice exports altered the incentives of agricultural producers. Suddenly there was an incentive to work more land and produce a larger crop than was necessary to feed one's family and pay taxes. Agriculture was commercialized by fiat, and in the absence of technical innovation and the availability of large quantities of easily cleared arable land, the area under cultivation increased rapidly.[16]

By the Fourth Reign land prices were already rising, at least in the Bangkok area.[17] By the Fifth Reign the growth of commercial agriculture seems to have led to still higher land values and to have sparked a commensurate interest in tightening what previously had been rather vaguely defined property rights. More attention was paid to demarcating precisely the boundaries of parcels of land, and creditors and *nai* began to accumulate land that was worked by their subordinates. The fundamental meaning and value of land underwent a major shift; while before land had been a means to support oneself, now it became a factor of production, providing landlords a way to accumulate wealth and power without having to chase after *phrai*. Land doesn't move, and landless farmers need landlords.

The second consequence of the Bowring Treaty was that it encouraged a substantial flow of money into the country in the form of precious metals. Siam had an export surplus for most of the period from the 1850s through 1910, and the balance was paid in silver. This accelerated the monetization of the economy. The demand for coinage was so great that the central government could not meet it, and the use of foreign coins was legalized in 1857, only two years after the Bowring Treaty.[18]

With more money in the economy, cash commutation of corvée and *suai* became increasingly popular among *phrai*. This development was encouraged by the central government, which had less use for *suai* following the decline of the Chinese junk trade and which found hired Chinese more reliable than corvée labor.

Commutation had the effect of depersonalizing the relationship between *nai* and *phrai*. If the *phrai* elected to commute their taxes, then the *nai* no longer had to

---

[14] Ingram, *Economic Change*, pp. 52-3. This may, however, reflect a low estimate of the total amount of production.

[15] Sompop, *Economic Development*, p. 49.

[16] Ingram, *Economic Change*, pp. 43-4, estimates that 5.8 million *rai* were planted to paddy in 1850, increasing to 11.5 million *rai* for the period 1910-1914. Sompop estimates slightly more than five million *rai* devoted to rice cultivation in 1860, increasing to over eight million by 1900, and nearly eleven million by 1910. Sompop, *Economic Development*, p. 51.

[17] "ประกาศเรื่องจำนำและขายฝากกรรมสิทธิ์ที่ดิน" ["Proclamation on Keeping and Selling Rights in Land"] in ประภาส จารุเสถียร รวบรวม, *ประชุมประกาศ ร. ๔* [Praphat Carusathian, ed., *Collected Proclamations of the Fourth Reign*] vol. 2, #238 (Bangkok: Memorial Volume for Phra Mahaphothiwongsacan Inthachothera, BE 2511), p. 282.

[18] Ingram, *Economic Change*, pp. 149-50, and M. R. Seni and M. R. Kukrit Pramoj, *A King of Siam Speaks* (Bangkok: Siam Society, 1987), pp. 49-52. The coins used were generally Mexican and Straits dollars, and Indian Rupiahs in the North.

delegate followers to do corvée nor did he have to assign them to produce *suai*. He simply had to pay the amount stipulated for the number of *phrai* for which he was registered. *Nai* became less like managers or foremen, and more like tax collectors. Monetization also provided a way to accumulate wealth and power without the burdensome task of collecting information on *phrai* and inducing them to cooperate.

The third consequence of the Bowring Treaty was the institution of extraterritoriality. This was the development that struck most directly at the manpower system. It essentially allowed European consuls to remove *phrai* from the system by making them protégés. This removed the *phrai* from certain tax obligations and from Siamese legal jurisdiction. It meant that *nai* could no longer use their followers in the traditional way; it severed the patronage relationship and made the consul the new patron for the *phrai*.

Missionaries similarly became, in effect, patrons for their converts. Converts were effectively removed from the traditional manpower system because the missionaries protested their recruitment for corvée labor and limited the kind of coercion that the *caos* could employ against them. Converts were frequently granted extraterritorial rights, or at least protégé status. This situation raised problems that continued to fester into the Fifth Reign.

Despite these difficulties, the relationships between *nai* and *phrai* did not simply evaporate. The strength of this decentralized system was precisely the adaptable nature of the personal bonds that held *nai* and *phrai* together. People steeped in the traditional political culture did not immediately change their behavior. They continued to operate with traditional schemata for hierarchy and authority, even as the changing economic environment began to make those schemata less useful and to make alternatives available. Many people, however, recognized that economic and social conditions were changing, and they actively began to seek new ways to think about power and new opportunities to satisfy traditional goals.

Political Reform and Foreign Ideas

There are a number of indications that Rama IV was interested in reforming the political system to centralize power. On several occasions he undertook efforts that paralleled the reform program later undertaken by his son. He streamlined the judicial process and took a more personal interest in appeals, for instance, an effort that Chulalongkorn later extended. This had the effect of giving him more control over *nai* when complaints were made against them.[19]

Rama IV also issued a proclamation urging officials not to concern themselves with affairs outside their official jurisdiction.[20] One might interpret this as an early plea for functional specialization, perhaps, but it was doomed to be ignored by unsalaried officials, who were difficult to discipline and had incentives to look out

---

[19] สภาลินี ขมะสุนทร, "แนวความคิดทางการเมืองของกลุ่มผู้นำในรัชสมัยพระบาทสมเด็จพระจุลจอม เกล้าเจ้าอยู่หัว ระหว่าง พศ ๒๔๐๐-๒๔๓๖" [Suphalini Khamasunthon, "The Political Thoughts of Elite Groups During the Reign of King Chulalongkorn BE 2400-2436"] (MA Thesis in History, Chulalongkorn University, BE 2528), pp. 39-40.

[20] "เตือนสติพนักงาน ต้องทำการเฉพาะตำแหน่ง" ["Warning Officials to Work Only in their Positions"] in ประภาส, *ประชุมประกาศ ร. ๔* [Praphat, *Collected Proclamations of the Fourth Reign*] vol. 1, #154, pp. 293-5.

for the interests of their clients and themselves rather than to respect jurisdictional boundaries. Functional specialization required radical changes in the structure and training of the bureaucracy, of the sort eventually undertaken under King Chulalongkorn.

Even more radically, Rama IV suggested switching from personalistic to territorial jurisdiction over *phrai*. He proposed that *nai* should be appointed for each village and *meuang*, and that when *phrai* moved, their registration should be transferred to the *nai* in the new village.[21] If anything came of this plan, it does not show up in the documents. Although seemingly straightforward, this scheme actually violated the central organizing principle of the old system. A similar plan implemented early in the Fifth Reign had disastrous consequences.[22]

Rama IV also hired foreign advisors to train elite military units in the "European style," although it is not entirely clear what that phrase meant.[23] Mongkut's *uparat*, Phraphinklao, also hired a foreign advisor to train his troops.

Rama IV was clearly interested in foreign ideas. He spoke English and Latin and had extensive contact with the foreign community in Bangkok, even engaging in theological debates with missionaries. His contact with the West was sporadic, however, and he never received the thorough education in European culture that his sons did. His interest in things European was never really matched by his opportunities.[24] Thus, despite a clear desire to reform the political system in ways for which European culture would have been a useful source of ideas, he did not have access to the same kind of intellectual resources that Chulalongkorn had as a result of the latter's education.

The education of the royal princes was of particular significance for the Fifth Reign. The education of princes had always been somewhat unusual, in that it was conducted in the palace rather than in a temple.[25] Most officials were taught to read and write using religious texts, and they then learned about politics by observing how others—their relatives or patrons—fulfilled their duties. The princes received a more sophisticated education. Tutors taught them history and statecraft, and the lessons they received in administration and politics as a result of firsthand experience in the palace were obviously of a special quality.

Chulalongkorn's early education was largely traditional, including tutoring in statecraft and history by his father, Rama IV. It departed from the traditional pattern in one important respect: he and some of his numerous brothers had American and

---

[21] จดหมายเหตุ ร. ๔ ๑๒๒๐/๕๕.

[22] Discussed below, p. 98.

[23] สมเด็จพระเจ้าบรมวงศ์เธอ กรมพระยา ดำรงราชานุภาพ, *ความทรงจำ* [Prince Damrong Rajanubhab, *Memories*] (Bangkok: Social Science Association of Thailand, BE 2505), pp. 104-5. Damrong points out that this was really part of a long tradition. The first Siamese king to hire European military experts was the seventeenth-century King Narai of Ayuthaya. See especially p. 136.

[24] According to Damrong, Rama IV wanted to travel to Singapore, but never had the opportunity because of his royal duties. Ibid., p. 164.

[25] วุฒิชัย มูลศิลป์, *การปฏิรูปการศึกษาในสมัยพระบาทสมเด็จพระจุลจอมเกล้าเจ้าอยู่หัว* [Wutichai Munsin, *The Reformation of Education in the Reign of King Chulalongkorn*] (Bangkok: Thai Wattana Panich, BE 2529), p. 9.

European tutors. During his minority this education continued, and he made two trips abroad to observe British and Dutch colonial administration, traveling to Singapore, Java, Malaysia, Burma, and India.[26] He also took lessons with Samuel Patterson, a tutor hired for the palace school Chulalongkorn set up for his younger brothers after his return from Singapore. By the early Fifth Reign most members of the court who were active in politics had some familiarity with—if not sympathy for—the West.[27] New schemata derived from the West were to have a profound effect on the shape of politics in the Fifth Reign.

THE FIFTH REIGN (1868-1910)

The demise of the old system in the Fifth Reign was internally generated; it was a revolution from above, carried out primarily in response to domestic problems. Such revolutions require resources, yet at the beginning of his reign Chulalongkorn commanded resources no better than—indeed, arguably inferior to—those of his predecessors. It is true that by the end of the Fifth Reign the throne had new resources to draw on, including a modern army, railroads and improved communications, and bureaucrats loyal to the throne. These were products of Chulalongkorn's reforms, however, not preconditions for them. When he became king, Chulalongkorn was politically weak, beholden to a powerful regent, with few supporters of his own, and he had little experience and no reputation. The core of the kingdom, the Central Plains, was in chaos, and the tax revenue that did reach the capital was siphoned off by rapacious officials, including the Regent himself.[28]

The Impetus for Reform

European colonialism is widely held to have stimulated reform in Siam by posing an external threat that prompted the King to reorganize his kingdom for stronger defense. I essentially agree with the argument that colonialism sparked reforms in Siam, however I will argue that the most significant stimulus was not so much the security threat; but rather the domestic impact of the new trade regime and exposure to a new set of schemata about politics.

It is not clear that the Siamese perceived an increased security threat from the British conquest of Burma. The Siamese and Burmese had been at war for centuries, on and off. In 1767 the Burmese completely annihilated Bangkok's predecessor, the Ayuthaya kingdom. It is hard to see how any security threat could be more severe than this. Some Siamese officials welcomed the British conquest of Burma on the grounds that it would improve the security of the kingdom.[29]

The major conflicts between Siam and colonial powers occurred only after the reform program was well underway. In the Northeast, conflicts with the French came after the Siamese began to assert control over areas of Laos and Cambodia,

---

[26] David Wyatt, *The Politics of Reform: Education in the Reign of King Chulalongkorn* (New Haven: Yale University Press, 1969), pp. 36-42.

[27] Ibid., p. 49.

[28] Royal income dropped precipitously during the Regency period, from 4.8 to 1.6 million baht annually in a five-year period. Tej Bunnag, *The Provincial Administration of Siam, 1892-1915: the Ministry of the Interior Under Prince Damrong Rajanubhab* (London: Oxford University Press, 1977), p. 12.

[29] ร ๕ รล-พษ ๓/๔๑๐, pp. 467-8.

tributaries where the Siamese had shared suzerainty with the Vietnamese. The most serious conflict with a Western power was an 1893 incident, in which a French gunboat breached Siamese defenses at the mouth of the Caophraya and steamed up to Bangkok. This was a traumatic event for the Siamese government, which was forced to renounce its claims to some territories along the Mekong. In some of these areas Siamese authority was tenuous, but in others it was quite concrete.[30] King Chulalongkorn was reportedly demoralized following this display, and he temporarily retired from public life. However, the gunboat incident occurred in 1893, after the reform program had begun. It may have helped reinforce support for that program among government officials, but it was not a cause of reform.

Internally, however, it seemed clear that the traditional system was in decline by the time Chulalongkorn ascended the throne in 1868. The economic changes altering the relationship between *nai* and *phrai* accelerated in the early Fifth Reign. Land rights became increasingly important; *nai* were rapidly being transformed into landlords, while *phrai* were becoming their tenants. The monetization of the economy made it more attractive for *phrai* to commute their traditional obligations to cash. All this had the effect of depersonalizing the relationship between *nai* and *phrai*.

In addition, the expansion of the "rice frontier" in the Central Plains led to the breakup of traditional villages and a "wild west" atmosphere in the newly opened rice lands. This made it more difficult to track and control people, and traditional administration became impossible in some areas.

What's more, colonial influences were infiltrating the kingdom. Missionary protégés continued to escape the control of traditional authorities. In the Northeast the French were very active in making Laotians into protégés, usually based on their conversion to Catholicism.[31] Protestant missionaries were less active in this respect: the Presbyterian mission baptized their first convert only after twelve years in the country.[32] Still, they were also perceived as a threat. The *cao* of Chiang Mai executed two Protestant converts before Bangkok forced him to be more accommodating. In the South missionaries appear to have been less of a problem. In the Fifth Reign Damrong was pleasantly surprised, on an inspection tour in Nakhon Si Thammarat, to find that missionaries there " . . . do not involve themselves in politics in any way."[33]

Siamese officials had difficulty detaining or trying protégés. As a result, foreign protégés enjoyed a comparative advantage in banditry. This, together with the

---

[30] On the territorial cession, the so-called "Scar of 1893," see Thongchai Winichakul, *Siam Mapped: A History of the Geo-Body of a Nation* (Honolulu: University of Hawai'i Press, 1994), pp. 141-50.

[31] ร. ๕ ม ๑.๔/๑๔.

[32] Missionary Samuel House, discussing this initial baptism, wrote that: " . . . so deep . . . was the duplicity of this people generally, and so many who professed interest in the teachings of the gospel had proved to be influenced by purely selfish motives, that when this case of genuine conviction of the truth occurred the brethren distrusted the sincerity of the man, and put him off from week to week." Samuel House, "History of the Missions in Siam and Laos," in *Siam and Laos as Seen by Our American Missionaries* (Philadelphia: Presbyterian Board of Publications, 1884), p. 380. The reluctance of the Protestants to make converts contrasted sharply with the aggressive style of the French Catholic missionaries, with the result that the Siamese government showed a marked preference for the Protestants and an antipathy for the French.

[33] ร. ๕ ม ๒.๑๔/๗๔.

erosion of *nai-phrai* relationships, the creation of new villages, and the increase of cash in circulation, caused banditry to flourish.

Increasing chaos meant that there was a certain impetus toward reform, but it was unclear at the time who might initiate that reform or what shape it would take. The only figure with the necessary authority to make radical institutional changes was the king, and yet he was in an extraordinarily weak political position at the time. Occupied by a young, inexperienced, and physically ill king deeply beholden to the Regent, the throne was almost the last place one would have expected to generate effective reforms.

Early Reforms

Despite their political weakness, Chulalongkorn and his brothers enjoyed an advantage as a result of their access to European ideas. Indeed, they had such ideas thrust upon them. In this they differed from more conservative elements in Thai society, such as the Bunnags, who dealt with Europeans when they had to but were not so interested in learning about European ways of understanding the world.

The position of the Bunnags was secure. They had little incentive to explore outside Thai culture because they were safely positioned at its height. In contrast, the position of the king and his brothers was far from secure despite their high birth. More or less at the mercy of the Bunnags, they not only appreciated more fully the challenges and opportunities presented by the West, they also had an incentive to change things.[34]

Internal Thai politics, not just the international situation, gave them an incentive to seek out non-traditional options. This made the "structure of the conjunction"[35] extremely favorable in the Siamese case. The king and his brothers were interested in exploring new ways of thinking about political organization and had access to foreign ideas. They discovered that the centralized model of the Weberian state— particularly in its absolutist colonial form—could be very useful for solving the problems they faced. This model also supplied a solution to the traditional problem of centralizing power without losing control over *phrai*. It provided a way to improve control over commoners as well as officials, centralizing power and making the king himself more directly the patron of all of his subjects. It gave the king and his

---

[34] Chulalongkorn was later to recall that " . . . the power of the ministers [i.e. the Bunnags] increased, because they had much more power to establish kings, until I became king. This was an unlucky time; as I was still a child, it was a great opportunity to reduce the power of the king completely, so I was like a kite with no more string to let out." A more idiomatic rendering of the last phrase in English might be "they had me on a short leash." "พระราชดำรัสตอบความเห็นของผู้จะให้เปลี่ยนการปกครอง จศ ๑๒๔๗" ["Royal Reply to the Views of Those Asking for a Change in Administration CS 1247"] in ชัยอนันต์ สมุทวณิช และ ขัตติยา กรรณสูต รวบรวม, *เอกสารการเมืองการปกครองไทย (พศ ๒๔๑๗ - ๒๔๗๗)* [Chai-anan Samudavanija and Khatthiya Kansut, ed., *Thai Political and Administrative Documents (BE 2417 - 2477)*] (Bangkok: Social Science Association of Thailand, BE 2532), p. 63.

[35] The phrase comes from Marshall Sahlins, *Islands of History* (Chicago: University of Chicago, 1985). It refers to the constellation of cultural, economic, and political forces on both sides of a contact situation, which combine to shape the actual events and behavior of the people and the groups that are meeting.

brothers the schematic resources to transform the *phrai* system into a modern, bureaucratic state responsive to the throne, and it outlined the foundations for a new state that might replace the old polity. At the same time, European imperialism provided additional motivation and justification for the enterprise.

This intellectual change brought a new way of conceptualizing power, one that made political centralization a practical goal for the king and spelled the doom of the old system of politics. Employing a European understanding of power, which measured power by one's control over territory exercised through bureaucratic authority and a monopoly of the use of legitimate violence, King Chulalongkorn was able to use the traditional authority and powers of the monarchy to assert his control at the grassroots level. In doing so he destroyed the old system and introduced the basic outlines of the structure of modern Thai politics.

The king's motivation in this matter was complex. The fact that the reforms secured his own power has led some to argue that this was his primary goal.[36] Chulalongkorn himself was careful to justify all his reforms in the name of progress, the happiness of the people, the improvement of the kingdom, or in traditional Buddhist terms. Some have taken these justifications at face value.[37] While it is impossible to reconstruct fully the motives of any person from historical evidence, it seems likely that Chulalongkorn's motives were a complex mix of these two positions. There is no evidence that he approached the reform process cynically. He really does seem to have believed that his policies were best for the people and Kingdom of Siam. Enacting those policies required him to secure his own power. It is probable that he did not try to disaggregate his motives any further than this.

On the other hand, other kings also probably believed that greater royal centralization would have been better for the kingdom. Rama I through Rama IV all fought military campaigns and undertook domestic reforms to this end. They were less successful in their domestic reforms due to differing circumstances, but also because they were engaged in the difficult enterprise of trying to invent ad hoc improvements in the only system of government they knew. Chulalongkorn had the advantage of exposure to a radically different and fully realized alternative model. For our purposes, the crucial point is that Chulalongkorn's education and circumstances supplied him with new conceptual resources unavailable to earlier kings.

Chulalongkorn's first reform efforts were piecemeal and tentative. There was substantial resistance to reform from the group of officials known as "Conservative Siam," who were led by the regent, Si Suriyawong.[38] As long as the regent and his allies held power in the capital, the king was unable to exert control over the central government.

The Bunnags, and in particular Si Suriyawong, dominated Bangkok and its environs in the early Fifth Reign. In addition, a conservative *uparat* was installed by the Bunnags at the same time that Chulalongkorn was selected as king. These people were siphoning off much of the substantial revenue generated by the traditional system of local government. While they controlled the central government, those

---

[36] See for instance Chatchai Panananon, "Siamese 'Slavery': the Institution and its Abolition" (PhD Dissertation, University of Michigan, 1982), pp. 182-5.

[37] For instance Chula Chakrabongse, *Lords of Life: A History of the Kings of Thailand* (London: Redman, 1967), Chapter 5.

[38] Wyatt, *Politics of Reform*, pp. 44-50.

resources were inaccessible to the king, and it was impossible to effect radical change.

Taking Control of the Central Government

In 1873 King Chulalongkorn came of age, and the Regency was terminated. *Caophraya* Si Suriyawong remained powerful, however, as was demonstrated by the early opposition to King Chulalongkorn's reform program, culminating in the Front Palace Incident of 1874-5.

Chulalongkorn initiated a series of reforms in the capital in 1873-5. This included, most importantly, a financial reform that centralized revenues somewhat and established an Audit Office.[39] A Finance Office was established in the palace that paid regular salaries to its employees and had a fixed place and fixed times of business. It was the first time such fundamental bureaucratic procedures had been employed in the Siamese government.[40] The effect was dramatic: in the first three years revenues to the throne increased by 36 percent.[41]

King Chulalongkorn officially abolished slavery in this period. This was accomplished by annually decreasing the price of manumission until the value reached zero. The immediate impact of this decree is ambiguous, and it is not clear how widely it was obeyed at the time. It was threatening to slaveholders, and to some slaves as well.[42] Chatchai has pointed out that, since freed slaves were to become *phrai luang*, the abolition of slavery would amount to a massive transfer of resources from the wealthy to the throne.[43] The gradual abolition was intended to reduce immediate opposition.

The king also established State and Privy Councils in 1874. The decrees that created these councils made extensive use of titles transliterated from English.[44] These were meant to be advisory bodies. The State Council was the more independent and powerful of the two, with the authority to meet independently of the king and to draft legislation. The Privy Council was a more informal group,

---

[39] The king personally inspected the accounts of this office. Wyatt, *Politics of Reform*, p. 54; and Wyatt, *Short History*, p. 197. Some central government revenue and all provincial revenue were outside its purview, however.

[40] สุมาลี บำรุงสุข, "การรวบรวมรายได้แผ่นดินในรัชกาลพระบาทสมเด็จพระจุลจอมเกล้าเจ้าอยู่หัว (พศ ๒๔๑๖-๒๔๕๓)" [Sumalee Bumroongsook, "The Consolidation of Government Revenue in the Reign of King Chulalongkorn (1873-1910)"] (MA Thesis in History, Chulalongkorn University, BE 2525), p. 79.

[41] In the previous three years they had decreased by roughly the same amount. Ibid., p. 77.

[42] See for instance David Bruce Johnston, "Rural Society and the Rice Economy in Thailand, 1880-1930" (PhD Dissertation, Yale University, 1975), pp. 102, 109. Johnston notes that emancipation threw onto their own resources some people who may have preferred a more secure, if more servile, existence as a debt slave. Chatchai argues that there was considerable resistance to emancipation among slaves as well as slave-owners. See Chatchai, "Siamese 'Slavery'," Chapter 5.

[43] Chatchai, "Siamese 'Slavery'," p. 225.

[44] Titles included "councilor," "clerk," "president," and so on. These have explanations attached in the decrees which formed the councils. เสถียร ลายลักษณ์ และคนอื่นๆ รวบรวม, *ประชุมกฎหมายประจำศก* [Sathian Lailak et al., eds., *Collected Laws*], vol. 8 (Bangkok: Daily Mail Printing House, BE 2478), pp. 170-83 and 185-91.

which might be called on to meet with the king on an ad hoc basis for the purpose of giving advice. Si Suriyawong was invited to join the Privy Council, but not the State Council. He refused in what must have been rather brusque terms, apparently upset that he had been asked to join the less important of the two bodies.[45] He and his supporters would in any case have been outnumbered in both councils by supporters of the king. Drawn from the group known as "Young Siam," the king's supporters tended to be hostile to the Regent. The Privy Council in particular became a forum for expressing disapproval of the current political order.[46]

The State Council and the Audit Office struck directly at Bunnag power by investigating and prosecuting Si Suriyawong's nephew, Nut, who was *Wang Na*. Nut was found guilty of misdirecting tax revenues collected by his office and of abusing his power. He was stripped of office, reduced to *phrai* status, and imprisoned.[47] This investigation was personally embarrassing to Si Suriyawong, not only because some of the embezzled funds had gone to him, but also because he was unable to protect a loyal follower. It must have alarmed other officials as well, since many could easily have been convicted of similar crimes.

These events—the abolition of slavery, the creation of the two new councils, the new financial institutions, and the prosecution of Nut—created a great deal of anxiety within "Conservative Siam," as well as the group called "Old Siam" made up of older officials who had served in earlier reigns and who were not necessarily members of the Bunnag faction. This anxiety culminated in the Front Palace Incident of 1874-5.

The Front Palace was the residence of the *uparat*, Prince Wichaichan, who seems to have felt his position threatened by the reforms of 1873-4 and by hostile speeches made by members of the Privy Council. These members complained that Wichaichan had been placed in his position in a highly irregular manner by Si Suriyawong.

Wichaichan may have thought this uproar indicated the King was going to remove him as *uparat*. He began gathering followers in the Front Palace, only yards from the Grand Palace, where the king lived. The king was alarmed in turn. In December 1874 relations broke down entirely, and the king placed troops around the Front Palace, virtually besieging it.[48] This gave the impression that a rebellion had broken out and created consternation in Bangkok. The sense of crisis deepened when mediation by Si Suriyawong failed, and the *uparat* sought British protection. The Governor of the Straits Settlement, Sir Andrew Clarke, made a grandstanding visit to Bangkok, but rather than assisting the *uparat* he claimed to have rescued Chulalongkorn. In fact, the final settlement was virtually identical to the one

---

[45] Si Suriyawong's letter to the king declining the invitation has been lost, but we do have a conciliatory response from Chulalongkorn indicating that the Regent claimed to have felt humiliated. This letter is reprinted in ณัฐวุฒิ สุทธิสงคราม, *สมเด็จเจ้าพระยาบรมมหา ศรีสุริยวงส์* [Natthawutthi Sutthisongkram, *Somdet Caophraya Borommaha Si Suriyawong*], vol. 1 (Bangkok: Si Tham, BE 2404), pp. 662-4.

[46] Wyatt, *Politics of Reform*, p. 56.

[47] Chatchai, "Siamese 'Slavery'," pp. 178-80.

[48] Noel Alfred Battye, "The Military, Government and Society in Siam, 1868-1910: Politics and Military Reform During the Reign of King Chulalongkorn" (PhD Dissertation, Cornell University, 1974), p. 181.

negotiated by Si Suriyawong except that Wichaichan was allowed to continue to reside in the Front Palace.[49]

The Front Palace Incident demonstrated the depth of opposition to the reforms of 1873-4 and the continued influence of the Regent. Various demonstrations of opposition to the reforms welled up during the crisis period, and the Privy Council—the "schoolboy council," as Si Suriyawong called it—came in for particular criticism.[50]

Reform slackened after the incident. The Councils were not formally dissolved, but they ceased to meet. The decade 1875-1885 constituted a lull in which most of the reforms of 1873-4 went unenforced. Despite the reduction of Wichaichan's powers, the conservatives had won the day.

Time, however, was on the side of the king. As Fourth Reign and Regency officials retired or died, he began replacing them with his own people, many of whom had been exposed to Western ideas through one of the Palace schools or through training in the Royal Pages.

King Chulalongkorn used this time to recruit and train loyal bureaucratic cadres. In 1878 an American missionary, Samuel McFarland, left his religious endeavors to found a modern school near Bangkok, with Siamese government support. The school taught Thai, English, the sciences, and mathematics. Scholarships were given to noble and royal pupils, although the bulk of the enrollment was made up of Chinese day-students who paid their own way.[51] The Royal Bodyguards, a branch of the Royal Pages, was also reorganized, and in 1881 a new school was created for them. Within a year admissions and the curriculum were expanded to make it into "a general training school for the bureaucracy."[52] Admissions were still restricted to those of "good birth," and the pool was small, mostly close relatives of the king.[53] The Royal

---

[49] The text of the agreement is available in Xie Shunyu, *Siam and the British, 1874-5: Sir Andrew Clarke and the Front Palace Crisis* (Bangkok: Thammasat University Press, 1988), pp. 65-7. Wichaichan's manpower was reduced to a two hundred-man bodyguard, and he lost all his political and financial authority; see p. 53. He retained only the title of *uparat* and the right to reside in the Front Palace.

[50] Battye, "The Military, Government and Society in Siam," pp. 194-5 and 207. Chulalongkorn noted in a personal letter that "The [Privy] Council is hated by many people," and implies, albeit obscurely, that Si Suriyawong may have been behind the whole affair. This letter is reprinted in ณัฐวุฒิ, *ศรีสุริยวงส์* [Natthawutthi, *Si Suriyawong*], vol. 1, pp. 767-71. See also Chatchai, "Siamese 'Slavery'," p. 230. If this is true, Si Suriyawong's goal would probably have been to exacerbate tensions between the king and the *uparat* to the degree that they would both need him to act as a mediator.

[51] David Wyatt, "Education and the Modernization of Thai Society," in *Change and Persistence in Thai Society: Essays in Honor of Lauriston Sharp*, ed. G. William Skinner and A. Thomas Kirsch (Ithaca: Cornell University Press, 1975), pp. 135-6.

[52] Wyatt, *Politics of Reform*, p. 105. It too used ranks and titles drawn from English. เสถียร, *ประชุมกฎหมายประจำศก ล. ๙* [Sathian, *Collected Laws, Vol. 9*], pp. 249-308.

[53] Damrong is quite explicit that the goal was to perpetuate the rule of "good families." สมเด็จพระเจ้าบรมวงศ์เธอ กรมพระยาดำรงราชานุภาพ, *เทศาภิบาล* [Prince Damrong Rajanubhab, *Thesaphiban*] (Bangkok: Memorial Volume for *Phraya* Atkrawisunthon, BE 2503), pp. 2-3.

Bodyguards provided a loyal core group that would be extremely important in the reforms to come.

Si Suriyawong and many of his most powerful supporters died between 1883 and 1886, allowing the king to appoint his own favorites to the positions that opened up as a consequence. While the king had political difficulties controlling or dislodging ministers once they were in office, no one challenged his authority to appoint whomever he pleased to those positions once they were vacated. His control over the central government thus increased slowly but steadily, and this set the stage for a second wave of reform.

In 1887 the king sent Prince Devawongse on a study trip to Europe to gather information on cabinet organization. On his return Devawongse recommended forming a cabinet with twelve functionally specialized ministries. Mock cabinet meetings were held for a while, to allow the king to test potential ministers and to allow everyone to familiarize himself with the system. In 1891 the plan became fully functional.[54]

The new cabinet retained the old Ministries of the Palace, the Capital, and Agriculture, and it included newly revamped Ministries of Finance and Foreign Affairs. The old Mahathai and Kalahom were retained. Initially the former dealt with *meuang* of the Central Plains, and the Northern and Northeastern tributaries, while the latter handled the South and the coastal *meuang*. Entirely new were the Ministries of Education, Public Works, Justice, the Privy Seal, and the Army.[55]

The creation of the new cabinet marked the beginning of serious and systematic reform. Many of the departments that had been nurtured and sheltered inside the Palace were now moved into the appropriate ministry, because the newer ministers were people trusted by the king rather than holdovers from the Regency period. The king was finally able to begin reshaping the central government in the bureaucratic image he desired.

At no point was the king's authority to make such changes challenged. Even during the height of opposition to reform, during the Front Palace crisis, no one ever claimed the king was legally bound to respect existing institutions and laws, though throughout the reform process there were people who opposed the particular changes he was making. The obstacles to reform had nothing to do with law or authority—they had to do with power. They were political, and by the late 1880s these political obstacles had been overcome.

Similarly, few objections were raised regarding the king's authority to alter the structure of provincial government. It was his prerogative to do so, and this seems to have been recognized by all. There were again political obstacles, but Chulalongkorn was able to overcome them, despite having begun his reign in such a weak position. There was little protest even from the nominally independent tributary states when Bangkok began to exercise increased power over them.

---

[54] Tej, *Provincial Administration*, pp. 60-1.

[55] เสถียร, *ประชุมกฎหมายประจำศก ล. ๑๒* [Sathian, *Collected Laws, Vol. 12*], pp. 93-8. The duties of the Mahathai and Kalahom were specialized two years later, when they were assigned their ancient mythical functions of Ministry of the Interior and of War, respectively. เสถียร, *ประชุมกฎหมายประจำศก ล. ๑๔* [Sathian, *Collected Laws, Vol. 14*], pp. 204-6.

Provincial Government

At the same time the king's reforms of provincial administration did encounter difficulties. In the late 1870s King Chulalongkorn attempted to use traditional local officials operating within the old Siamese political culture in a reform experiment similar to one proposed by his father. The result was a disaster, but for reasons which are instructive.

Some time prior to 1878 an attempt was made to shift the administration of some *meuang* in the Northeast from a personalistic to a territorial basis. *Phrai* were allowed to move freely and pay taxes wherever they lived. As Chulalongkorn himself explained some years later,

> Originally when a *phrai* in one *meuang* moved his home to another *meuang*, the *nai* from the old *meuang* still had to contact him for his taxes, which was difficult. So the idea was that we wouldn't tattoo *phrai* from the Lao *meuang*; if a *phrai* chose not to live in one town and moved to another, then for instance if he had to pay *suai* in the old *meuang*, now he would pay in the new town. This idea was aimed at people who moved to new *meuang*—it was never meant to allow people living in this *meuang* to choose to be under the authority of that one.[56]

What actually happened, however, is that people took the opportunity to move wherever they could get the best deal. *Nai* remained lax about reporting the *phrai* under their control, and the new policy gave them a better excuse than ever to remove *phrai* from the rolls. The net result was that *phrai* disappeared at a greater rate than before. When royal commissioners were sent to the area to clear up the problem, bitter conflicts developed between competing *nai*.[57] The *phrai* system in parts of the Northeast seems never to have recovered.[58]

Territorially defined authority could only work in conjunction with other reforms. It required officials responsive to the central government and trained in a different way of conducting business. They had to allow themselves to be bound by the rules and laws of the central government and to see their responsibilities and careers as tied to Bangkok. Such officials would have to collect information, report back to Bangkok on a regular basis, and administer policy in a standardized way across discrete territories defined by mapping. They would have to become bureaucrats.

Modern bureaucracy evolved in Europe through centuries of painful trial and error. The Siamese had the advantage of a fully worked out model in the form of European colonial administrations, but even so, implementing that model required freeing up resources for salaries and training people in specialized skills such as mapping, accounting, standardized record-keeping, census-taking, and so on. The solution was available, but there was a lot to learn first. Furthermore, as Westney points out with respect to Meiji Japan, imitating alien institutions requires innovation because they must be made to function in a new context.[59] Until this intellectual

---

[56] ร. ๕ บ ๑.๒/๙ ร. ที่ ๕๒๑/๙๖.

[57] ร. ๕ รล-พษ ๓/๑๓๑, pp. 142-3.

[58] Ibid., ร. ๕ รล-พษ ๓/๑๙๘, pp. 172-3 and ร. ๕ บ ๑.๒/๒๘ ร ที่ ๑๙๕/๕๐.

[59] D. Eleanor Westney, *Imitation and Innovation: The Transfer of Western Organizational Patterns to Meiji Japan* (Cambridge, MA: Harvard University Press, 1987), p. 6.

infrastructure could be built, a European-style territorial bureaucracy could not work, and the King had to be more or less content to operate within the old system.[60]

Through the 1880s King Chulalongkorn took advantage of opportunities to consolidate his control over the tributary states of the North and Northeast, sending resident commissioners to some of them. In part this was done to centralize authority, and in part it was done to claim for Siam those areas whose status might have been ambiguous because certain tributary states owed allegiance to more than one great power. In particular the king wanted to pre-empt French claims to the Lao states.[61]

In 1880 a British surveyor, James Fitzroy McCarthy, was hired to survey the borders of Siam. This was important particularly for countering French claims to the Lao states. McCarthy trained his own assistants, and he helped to establish a survey school in 1882 and the Royal Survey Department in 1885. The territorial dimension of the coming reforms would depend heavily on mapping the areas in question.[62]

Systematic provincial reform was begun only in 1892, when Prince Damrong became Mahathai. Damrong was the very model of the new bureaucratic cadre that the king was trying to create. He was a younger brother of Chulalongkorn, an alumnus of the Royal Pages school and later head of the Royal Bodyguards school, and he had recently returned from a study trip in Europe. His knowledge of European methods of administration appears to have justified his promotion over several older brothers.[63]

Damrong recorded that he spent his first year observing the workings of the Ministry without making great changes. However, during this period he did something no other minister in living memory had done: he toured the provinces under his charge. He later gleefully recounted the consternation this caused among provincial officials, who were at a loss to comprehend it.[64]

In 1894 the Mahathai became the Ministry of the Interior, assuming control of the Southern *meuang* from the Kalahom, which became the Ministry of War. Damrong reorganized the Ministry of the Interior and embarked on the program of provincial reform that became known as "Thesaphiban."[65]

---

[60] Territorial reform in the Northeast was not brought up again until 1895, as the intellectual infrastructure described above was gradually being created. See ร. ๕ ม ๑.๔/๑๔.

[61] Kennon Breazeale, "The Integration of the Lao States into the Thai Kingdom" (PhD Dissertation, Oxford University, 1975), Chapter 8.

[62] James McCarthy, *Surveying and Exploring in Siam* (London: John Murray, 1900); and Thongchai, *Siam Mapped*, pp. 283-6.

[63] On the occasion of Damrong's promotion, the king said that: " . . . it is necessary to know about European methods of administration because the Europeans are hundreds of times more experienced than we are in this activity, so we must employ someone who knows about these methods, to lay down the new administrative regulations." Tej, *Provincial Administration*, p. 86.

[64] ดำรง, *เทศาภิบาล* [Damrong, *Thesaphiban*], pp. 18-23.

[65] This appears to be a neologism coined for the occasion. The term does not appear in Pallegoix's 1854 lexicon, *สัพะพะจะนะ พาสาไทย* / *Dictionarium Linguae Thai Sive Siamensis* (Paris: Jussu Imperatoris Impressum, 1854); or in D. B. Bradley's 1873 Thai dictionary, หนังสือ อักขราภิธานศรับท์ / *Dictionary of the Siamese Language* (Bangkok, 1873 [facsimile edition by Khurusapha Press, Bangkok, BE 2514]). It is a compound derived from the Sanskrit *desa*,

Thesaphiban evolved over the years through a series of decrees, ministerial circulars, and local experiments. The system was extended gradually between 1894 and 1900, expanding a few provinces at a time. It had to be implemented and extended slowly because of a chronic shortage of qualified personnel. This slow pace, however, had the advantage of making the transition to the new system less abrupt.

The basic model for Thesaphiban was British Burma. Siamese officials undertook a number of study trips to various European countries and colonies in the 1880s, but information about Burma was particularly widely circulated. The institutional structure of Thesaphiban adhered very closely to that of British Burma.[66] Siam was territorially subdivided into administrative circles (*monthon*), *meuang*, districts (*amphoe*), communes (*tambon*), and villages (*mu ban*). As in Burma, these were administrative conveniences, or constructs, with little correspondence to any natural feature or pattern of settlement.

Each level down to the *amphoe* was governed by a salaried official appointed by Bangkok. These officials were expected to act according to explicit standards and rules of conduct set in the capital, were accountable to their superiors, could be promoted and demoted based on their performance, and could be dismissed. Their authority was defined territorially, and their powers were restricted to the functions they served. The authority to use violence was restricted to police and army units operating on the authority of their superiors. They were, in other words, bureaucrats.[67]

High-status appointees from Bangkok filled most of the top leadership positions in this new order; many of them had been educated at the various schools set up by the king.[68] These schools were small and underfunded, and consequently there was a

---

meaning area or territory, and *abhipala*, meaning to protect or guard. This is rendered in Thai as *thesa* + *aphiban*. Thongchai hence translates it as "protection over territory," drawing a contrast with the old system in which territory was relatively unimportant. Thongchai, *Siam Mapped*, p. 103.

[66] Reports about British administration in Burma were given special prominence in *Wachiriyan*, a journal circulated among educated central Thai elites with an interest in politics and foreign affairs. Numbers 6-8 reported on the Burmese legal system; 9, 22, and 24 on general administrative structure; 11 and 14 on tax policy; and 15-21 on the police. Numbers 10, 12, and 13 contained articles on British indirect rule in Northern Malaya. No articles appeared on Dutch Java or French Indochina. The above articles claim to be based on firsthand observation and appeared between March 1884 and December 1886.

[67] Following Weber's classic definition, in *Economy and Society*, vol. I, ed. Guenther Roth and Claus Wittich (Berkeley: University of California Press, 1978), pp. 220-1.

[68] Chulalongkorn preferred candidates who were qualified by education to those who were not so qualified, but he would have welcomed an increase in the number of aristocratic candidates with the requisite education, since he preferred them to highly trained commoners. See, for instance, Wyatt, "Education and Modernization," pp. 137-9, which cites decrees by the king encouraging both royalty and the children of nobles and prominent officials to acquire the education that would qualify them for bureaucratic appointment. The new administration did draw on commoners, lesser nobility, and Chinese, who responded more readily than the elite to the opportunities provided by these new forms of education. This prompted concern on the part of the king that members of the nobility were cutting themselves off from political power or relying excessively on personal connections for jobs. Scholarships and preference for places in the government-sponsored schools were aimed at the children of the elite in an attempt to reverse this trend.

chronic shortage of manpower.[69] Officials from Bangkok were generally forced to recruit their staff locally in the provinces, and they often chose people from prominent local families or traditional local officials. This had the accidental benefit of helping to smooth the way for the transition by co-opting traditional community leaders into the system. Opposition among local officials was thus reduced, and the association between traditional, hierarchical merit and power was perpetuated at the local level. Some of the legitimacy of the new order was thus attached to the old.

Tambon and village officials were elected locally—as in Burma—but had to be approved by bureaucrats appointed in Bangkok. They were also often drawn from the pool of traditional local officials.

Traditional local officials were hurt most by the reforms, and their lack of resistance demands some explanation. The reforms reduced the scope of their authority and removed most of the politically generated rents from which they had derived their resources. Co-opting some of these people into the new order helped reduce opposition to it, but even so the transition was remarkably peaceful, particularly as compared to the process of centralization in European states and their colonies.

In both Europe and the colonies, local officials who lost influence and resources through the centralization of power that inevitably accompanied modern state formation resisted with violence.[70] In Siam, by contrast, there was remarkably little violent opposition to the centralization of power. Some traditional officials appear to have supported the 1901-2 "Holy Man's" rebellion that broke out among the Kha in the Northeast.[71] Some may also have been involved in a Shan rebellion in the North in 1902.[72] In the South uncooperative *caos* were removed and exiled to Bangkok by

---

[69] Ibid., p. 141. Enrollments remained approximately the same between 1885 and 1898, despite enormous growth in the bureaucracy. This reflected budgetary politics.

[70] See for instance Otto Hintze, "Military Organization and the Organization of the State," in *Historical Essays of Otto Hintze*, ed. Felix Gilbert (New York: Oxford University Press, 1975), pp. 192-215; Charles Tilly, ed., *The Formation of National States in Western Europe* (Princeton: Princeton University Press, 1975); and Charles Tilly, *Coercion, Capital and European States, AD 990-1990* (Cambridge: Basil Blackwell, 1990).

[71] John Murdoch, "1901-2 'Holy Man's' Rebellion," *Journal of the Siam Society* 62,1 (1974): 61-2. One of the leaders of the movement was a disgruntled aspirant to the position of *cao meuang* of Khukan. นงลักษณ์ ลิ้มศิริ, "ความสำคัญของกบฏหัวเมืองอีสาน พศ ๒๓๒๕ - ๒๔๔๕" [Nonglak Limsiri, "The Significance of the Rebellions in the Northeastern Provinces of Thailand BE 2325 – 2445"] (MA Thesis in History, Chulalongkorn University, BE 2524), p. 90. Bangkok officials were deeply suspicious that the *cao* of the plundered town of Khemerat had not resisted the "Holy Men" (ร. ๕ ม ๒.๑๘/๓), and one commented that the "Holy Men" were most successful in areas where the power of the old *caos* and religion had declined. ร. ๕ ม ๒.๑๘/๑๑. See also เตช บุนนาค, ขบถ รศ ๑๒๑ [Tej Bunnag, *The Revolts of RS 121*] (Bangkok: Thai Wattana Panich, BE 2524), Chapters 2 and 3.

[72] Shan bandits had been a problem in the North for some time, partly because the Shan were particularly hurt by the political reform. The town of Phrae was attacked in a peculiar and specific pattern, however. The bandits cut the telegraph line, raided central government offices and the jail, and then hunted down and killed central Thai officials. All other property—Northern Thai, Shan, and European—went conspicuously untouched. The *cao*

central Thai officials arriving on a gunboat.[73] In none of these three cases did the *caos* openly oppose the Bangkok government, nor did complaints arise that the government had exceeded its authority in dealing swiftly and decisively with the threat.[74]

Kings had always had the authority to remove *caos* and to oversee the *meuang*. If previous kings had not done so on a regular basis, it was because they had not considered the practice to be especially beneficial or profitable. They had interfered at the local level only occasionally, when there was a compelling reason to do so. As long as politics was based on the control of manpower, however, it made sense for kings to allow local leaders autonomy. Now that new bureaucratic techniques allowed the king to centralize power, and the creation of something that Europeans would recognize as good government became valuable in foreign relations, it was in the king's interest to alter the system. The relative ease with which he did so points to the resources other kings could have mustered to that end, if they had seen it as productive.

What changed in the Fifth Reign was that a new way of thinking about politics — new schemata — became available to the king, allowing him much tighter control over local officials by basing authority on territorial control. This represented a profound change in Siamese political culture, changing old institutions and habits, but it was a change that kings always had the authority and the power to make. What they had lacked were not material resources, but conceptual ones.

Local officials essentially faced a choice between accepting the new system or losing their political positions. The changing economic environment already made the *nai-phrai* relationship more problematic. Now the changing institutional framework undermined those relationships further. With the increased centralization of authority and the standardization of rules across districts, the traditional *nai* were increasingly unable to defend their clients against the central government, and they therefore became less attractive as patrons. As districts were demarcated and an administrative grid was laid down, it began to make little difference where *phrai* resided or who their *nai* was, as all were subject to the same standardized rules. As power was transferred to central government bureaucrats, it increasingly made sense for *phrai* to look to them, rather than to traditional local leaders, as patrons. It

---

meuang refused to help the Siamese commissioner and fled to French Laos after the incident. See Ansil Ramsay, "Modernization and Reactionary Rebellions in Northern Siam," *Journal of Asian Studies* 38,2 (1979): 283-97; ร. ๕ ม ๖๓/๓ and ๖๓/๑๐. After the rebellion, the highest-ranking *caos* of the Northern tributaries were exiled to Bangkok. The same year the Ministry of the Interior opened a school in the North to train the sons of "good families" to take up roles in the new administration. See ร. ๕ ม ๕๘/๕๑ ฟัก ๕๒.

[73] ร. ๕ ม ๗๖/๕; เทช, ขบถ [Tej, *Revolts*], Chapter 3; and Tej, *Provincial Administration*, pp. 152-3.

[74] It should be noted that some local officials also took the traditional option of flight; they generally fled to French colonies and often took with them a substantial following. This option, however, required the refugees to live under a colonial hegemony no more attractive than that of Bangkok, and some of these officials returned to Siam. See for instance ร. ๕ ม ๒.๖๕/๕-๗, ๖๕/๒๗-๒๘, ๕๗/๑๓, ๕๘/๑๓, ๒๐๘.

therefore also made sense for *nai* to find positions in the new bureaucratic hierarchy, so as to maintain their positions as patrons and leaders.

The Conservation of Tradition

Even as these changes took place, the reforms of King Chulalongkorn conserved much of the traditional Siamese political culture in a way that made the process of change proceed more smoothly. As discussed above, many local officials were carried over from the old system. The Sangha was also preserved and centralized. Because these changes emanated from the throne, the monarchy was obviously to be retained.

The co-optation of local officials helped defuse local resistance to reform by depriving it of leadership, but it also helped to transfer some of the karmic authority of the old regime to the new. Because those recognized as superiors in the old system were willing to work for the new, it acquired some of the legitimacy of the old.

Religious sources of legitimacy were also turned to the support of the new system. The Sangha had traditionally been very decentralized, but the central government began to create a religious bureaucracy linking village temples to Bangkok.[75] The 1902 Sangha Act created a hierarchy of religious officials that paralleled the civil service hierarchy. All monks were required to be attached to a temple, and some were rewarded with bureaucratic positions that included "offerings" — in effect salaries — in cash. The king personally supervised the appointment of the highest-ranking religious officials, and these in turn supervised the appointment of lower-level officials down to the abbots of village temples.[76]

Kings had always been responsible for periodic purifications of the Sangha, and these changes could easily be represented in that tradition.[77] They also had the effect of giving the Buddhist clergy incentives to support the reform. Since monks were often influential local leaders, this was also a powerful source of legitimacy for the new system. The central government even experimented with using village temples as the infrastructure of a national educational system.[78]

The reforms also perpetuated the role of the monarchy. This is hardly surprising given that the monarch was the originator of the reforms. In 1885 a group of Siamese students educated in Europe suggested to the king that he should create a constitutional monarchy with a parliament and circumscribed role for the throne, exactly the kind of regime predominant in Europe at the time. Chulalongkorn replied

---

[75] See Craig Reynolds, "The Buddhist Monkhood in Nineteenth-Century Thailand" (PhD Dissertation, Cornell University, 1972); and Kamala Tiyavanich, *Forest Recollections: Wandering Monks in Twentieth-Century Thailand* (Honolulu: University of Hawai'i Press, 1997), Chapters 7 and 8.

[76] Yoneo Ishii, *Sangha, State and Society: Thai Buddhism in History*, trans. Peter Hawkes (Honolulu: University of Hawai'i Press, 1986); and Somboon Suksamran, *Political Patronage and Control Over the Sangha* (Singapore: Institute of Southeast Asian Studies, Research Notes and Discussion Papers #28, 1981), pp. 31-4.

[77] Ishii, *Sangha, State and Society*, p. 51; and Tambiah, *World Conqueror and World Renouncer: A Study of Buddhism and Polity in Thailand Against a Historical Background* (New York: Cambridge University Press, 1976), Chapters 5 and 11.

[78] The effort was abandoned due to a lack of resources and support at the local level. See Tambiah, *World Conqueror and World Renouncer*, pp. 219-25; and Wyatt, *Politics of Reform*, pp. 233-55.

that the time was not yet right for democracy in Thailand, and that monarchy was still a more appropriate system.[79]

In Siam there was remarkably little agitation for a total rejection of tradition, as occurred, for instance, in Japan and China. Political change seems, even for those radicals calling for a constitutional regime, to have been the legitimate purview of the king. Without a strong monarchy, it is unlikely that reform in Siam would have succeeded, or that the kingdom would have remained independent. With the king as its champion, holding the undisputed power to make deep political changes, reform had at least some chance of success.

---

[79] The complete text of this exchange is available in ชัยอนันต์ และ ขัตติยา รวบรวม, *เอกสาร* [Chai-anan and Khatthiya, ed., *Documents*], pp. 31-67. Chulalongkorn's response is rather indirect, beginning with an account of his struggle against the Bunnags in his early reign. He claims to have filled the role of an "opposition" during this period. He also accepts that it would be useful to have assistance with legislative matters, and bemoans the lack of qualified people to help him. He then goes on to claim that Siam needs a number of reforms before it can have an elected legislature. For another suggestion that Siam become a parliamentary democracy, see เทียนวรรณ, "ไปรเวตคำแนะนำ" [Thianwan, "Private Introduction"] in the same volume, pp. 120-1.

Chapter 6

CONCLUSION:
CULTURE AND POWER
IN A COMPARATIVE PERSPECTIVE

Treating Siam in isolation obscures the significance of the case. Looking at the kingdom in a comparative perspective helps to highlight how unusual its experience was and to locate the importance of both power and culture in state formation. This chapter will therefore begin by briefly comparing Siam to Burma and Japan. This comparison is followed by a summary of the interplay between culture and choice in the Siamese case, concluding with an assessment of the relationship between culture and power.

BURMA AND JAPAN: COMPARATIVE CASES

An early nineteenth-century observer might well have thought Burma more likely to succeed at adopting the institutions of the modern state than Siam. More centralized than Siam, and threatened more directly by European imperialists, Burma had numerous incentives to reform along lines that Europeans would recognize as good government. Yet its reform efforts failed.

The Burmese kingdom resembled a more centralized version of Siam. It was quite similar culturally to Siam. The core Burman[1] population was Theravada Buddhist, with religious practices and beliefs similar to the Thai. The kingdom also incorporated non-Burman minority groups, just as the Siamese kingdom included non-Thai minorities. Territory played a larger role in political life, however, because of the greater importance of irrigation for agriculture in the core area of the kingdom, Upper Burma.[2] This tended to fix the population more firmly on the ground and gave the central government more access to local resources.

King Mindon (r. 1852-1878) initiated a reform effort in Burma following the second Anglo-Burmese war. He undertook a number of initiatives, including hiring foreign advisors, importing European weapons and steamships, dispatching students abroad to study, educating his own children in English and French, and opening

---

[1] I use "Burmese" here to refer to the entire population of the Kingdom of Burma, regardless of ethnicity. "Burman" refers to the majority Buddhist, Burmese-speaking ethnic group.

[2] Michael Aung-Thwin, *Irrigation in the Heartland of Burma: Foundations of the Pre-Colonial Burmese State* (DeKalb: Northern Illinois University Center for South and Southeast Asian Studies, Occasional Paper #15, 1990), pp. 5-7.

diplomatic relations with several Western powers. His heir apparent, Prince Kanaung, was put in charge of the development of model factories.[3]

The reform effort came too late, however. After the second Anglo-Burmese War of 1852, the Burmese throne was deprived of crucial resources by the British annexation of the southern part of the country. Mindon's modernization program and the ordinary costs of government had to be paid out of a reduced pool of resources. The leasing of teak concessions to foreign firms and attempts to introduce a new tax system failed to generate sufficient new revenues, and a scheme to convert many officials' salaries to cash floundered as a result.[4]

The problem of insufficient resources was compounded by weak leadership. The model factories of Prince Kanaung languished after his assassination in 1866.[5] After Mindon died in 1878, royal support for the reform faltered. Although the reform faction was instrumental in picking King Mindon's successor, King Thibaw, he did not consistently support them in return. The new king was inexperienced and pliable, and he lacked strong leadership skills.[6] As other court factions maneuvered for influence, the reformers lost control, and Thibaw's reign degenerated into a series of coups and counter-coups, plots and massacres.[7]

Thus, the structure of the conjunction was unfavorable in Burma. There was an impetus for reform, and while some officials did begin to acquire the information and skills necessary to build a modern state, the throne no longer had adequate resources to support this effort. Although Burma started out in a more advantageous position than Siam, by the time reform began the government was already starved for resources.

Japan, on the other hand, is a success story, like Siam. A relatively minor power in the traditional Asian political order, it managed to fend off imperialism through a series of reforms that created a new government modeled on the modern state. Indeed, Japan has become a classic case of revolution from above in the comparative social science literature.[8]

The literature on the Meiji Restoration consistently cites two reasons for its success: the high level of resources available to the reformers, and their explicit adoption of European organizational models, be they in industry, the military, or

---

[3] See Myo Myint, "The Politics of Survival in Burma: Diplomacy and Statecraft in the Reign of King Mindon, 1853-1878" (PhD Dissertation, Cornell University, 1987); Oliver Pollak, *Empires in Collision: Anglo-Burmese Relations in the Mid-Nineteenth Century* (Westport: Greenwood Press, 1979), pp. 13, 117 and 120-2; and John F. Cady, *A History of Modern Burma* (Ithaca: Cornell University Press, 1958), pp. 101-2.

[4] The salary scheme had little political support anyway, because it would have reduced the income of the officials affected. Myint, "Politics of Survival," Chapter 5.

[5] Pollak, *Empires in Collision*, p. 127.

[6] Paul J. Bennett, *Conference Under the Tamarind Tree: Three Essays in Burmese History* (New Haven: Yale Southeast Asia Series #15, 1971), pp. 71-3.

[7] The story of Thibaw's rather depressing reign is told in Charles Lee Keeton, *King Thebaw and the Ecological Rape of Burma: the Political and Commercial Struggle between British India and French Indo-China in Burma, 1878-1886* (Delhi: Manohar Book Service, 1974).

[8] See for instance Barrington Moore, *The Social Origins of Dictatorship and Democracy: Lord and Peasant in the Making of the Modern World* (Boston: Beacon Press, 1966), Chapter 5; Reinhard Bendix, *Kings or People: Power and the Mandate to Rule* (Berkeley: University of California Press, 1978), Chapter 12; or Theda Skocpol, *States and Social Revolutions: A Comparative Analysis of France, Russia, and China* (New York: Cambridge University Press, 1979), pp. 99-104.

government.[9] As in Siam, cultural change coincided with the changing control of resources.

The Tokugawa regime, which ruled Japan from 1600 to 1868, evolved from a feudal organization into a quasi-bureaucratic one. The samurai were gradually removed from their fiefs and instead were paid salaries by their lords. Eventually the great domains of the *daimyo* were run by salaried samurai who were selected and promoted by merit as much as birth.[10] The *daimyo* themselves remained the last feudal element in the system, holding their domains by hereditary tenure. However, they were also increasingly impoverished by the Tokugawa policy that required the *daimyo* to maintain a residence in the capital, something that led them to press their samurai to develop and extract more resources from their domains.

The samurai who overthrew the Tokugawa regime in 1868 were drawn from this class of bureaucratized samurai. Operating in the name of the Meiji Emperor, they succeeded in retiring the *daimyo* and tying the domains into a centralized structure of government. This process was considerably more violent than in Siam, as the *daimyo* resisted, and a series of civil wars and rebellions resulted. In the end, however, the new government came to command considerable resources, which were employed for a radical program of political reform designed explicitly to strengthen the country against foreign attack and to remove the unequal treaty provisions.

Although the Japanese government's subsequent success in promoting industrialization has led many social scientists to treat the Meiji Restoration as the classic case of revolution from above, in a sense the Siamese case is even more remarkable. The political transformation of Siam was effected in a profoundly conservative way. There was little violence and no radical revision of the class system. The political conflicts that surrounded the reform effort were concentrated in the capital and were the same sorts of conflicts that characterized the old political system: those between king and *uparat*, the throne and the nobility, and Bangkok and the *meuang*. Even the goals of the reform were traditional in nature: they sought to centralize power without losing control of *phrai*. What was revolutionary in Siam were the new techniques—not the goals or the actors—the king deployed, based on schemata drawn from European culture.

In Siam, King Chulalongkorn was able to do what Siamese monarchs had always aspired to do, but had never been able to achieve. He was able to centralize power and make local officials responsive to the throne. Yet he began his reign as one of the weakest of the Chakri kings: young, ill, with little experience and few allies. How was this possible?

CULTURE AND CHOICE

Part of the answer is that he had access to a fully worked out and tested alternative model in the form of European colonial administration, particularly the British administration in Burma. This model introduced new schemata that pointed him in radical new directions unexplored by earlier Siamese kings.

---

[9] For instance, Thomas Smith, *The Agrarian Origins of Modern Japan* (Stanford: Stanford University Press, 1959); Ronald Dore, *Education in Tokugawa Japan* (Berkeley: University of California Press, 1965); and D. Eleanor Westney, *Imitation and Innovation: The Transfer of Organizational Patterns to Meiji Japan* (Cambridge, MA: Harvard University Press, 1987).

[10] On the bureaucratization of the samurai, see Thomas Smith, *Native Sources of Japanese Industrialization, 1750-1920* (Berkeley: University of California Press, 1988), pp. 138-40.

Yet precisely because of the traditional authority of Thai kings, the reforms could be justified by tradition. The reform of the Sangha evoked traditional royal obligations to preserve and support Buddhism even as the institution was being brought under central control for the first time. The provincial reform involved recruiting local elites—who were needed to help address the manpower shortage—and thus drew on their traditional legitimacy at the local level. The fact that the reform emanated from the throne preserved and used the traditional karmic supremacy of the king. Karmic hierarchy was retained at all levels of the reform to continue to legitimate power and justify change.

Because of these continuities, there was minimal cognitive shock to most Thais. Indeed, in many respects the reform could actually be represented as a return to tradition in a rapidly changing world. The generally conservative cast of Thai politics since this time is doubtless related to the cultural continuity of this revolution from above.

At the same time, radically new schemata became relevant to government officials. Knowledge of law, bureaucratic regulations, official duties, technical skills, mathematics and the writing of reports all became critical. New habits needed to be developed. Working for a salary, keeping office hours, respecting territorial boundaries, and interacting in a bureaucratic hierarchy were all habits that required the mastery of new schemata, now necessary if a person aspired to be successful in a government career.

CULTURE AND POWER

Ideas alone were not sufficient. Implementing them required resources. Both power and authority were required. Many powerful people, including the key local officials who held the system together, as well as important officials of the central government, had interests that were hurt by the reforms. Chulalongkorn's revolution from above had to overcome these objections.

The most successful centralizers, the European absolutist monarchs, had overcome the resistance of local authorities and privileged nobles through coercion. In other non-European settings, many kings whose situations resembled that of the Thai monarchs had attempted similar reforms, but failed due to domestic resistance—the Qing dynasty in China during the Hundred Days Reform, for instance, or King Mindon in Burma. How could Chulalongkorn succeed when these monarchs, often with more wealth and power than he, had failed?

The standard interpretation of Thai kings as politically weak compounds the puzzle. If Thai kings were generally weak, it seems even less likely that a young, ill, and inexperienced king like Chulalongkorn could transform the kingdom and make himself, in effect, an absolute monarch. Chulalongkorn was a talented leader, armed with ideas that were radically new, but even so he needed the resources necessary to put those ideas into effect and followers who supported him as he sought to exercise that leadership. How could the weakest of a weak line find these resources?

The answer, I would argue, is that Siamese kings had always possessed such resources. One key resource was their supreme position in the karmic hierarchy that defined social relations within Siam. They could also make new laws and change the institutional structure of the government. While they might face political difficulties and resistance, they also had considerable capacity to enforce their decisions. The taxes and labor they extracted through the *phrai* system were considerable. The most important political limitations they faced involved officials in the capital. When the interests of the court and the king coincided, they could muster formidable forces.

In this context, the decentralization of power and delegation of authority to local officials should not be taken as evidence of weakness. It could actually be perceived as a key component of the king's power. To understand how, we need to understand what Thai kings were trying to do, and how they understood the opportunities available to them. For this purpose, it is necessary to interpret the concepts or schemata with which people understood their world. When we do this, decentralization can be understood as a reasonable—even rational—strategy for someone operating with schemata drawn from traditional Siamese political culture.

The most important schema for understanding political life in the early Bangkok period involved karma and its relationship to power. The Siamese understood people to be intrinsically unequal, with some more effective, lucky, and insightful than others. This difference was explained by karma: merit and demerit accumulated through past actions. Karmic inferiors should spontaneously recognize the merit of their superiors, looking to them for assistance. The size and loyalty of a person's following was evidence of his merit and status. Thus karma mapped onto political power. Superiors needed the resources their followers provided to sustain their power and their claim to karmic superiority, while inferiors in this highly unequal society benefited from the patronage of superiors. Power was thus intensely personalistic in this system. It emerged from the specific relationship between individual *nai* and *phrai*. Higher levels of government built on this relationship and had to respect it to maintain the integrity of the system.

The cultural logic of this system militated against excessive centralization. Because the *phrai* system rested on personal connections between leaders and followers, the system had to give *nai* the autonomy to handle those relationships as they saw fit. To do otherwise would have driven both *nai* and *phrai* out of the system. Thai kings would have liked to wield more precise control over the kingdom, but prudence and common sense required them to accept that they had to work through intermediaries. As with political leaders everywhere, they had to accept that they could not have things exactly as they wanted them, that they had to make tradeoffs.

Centralization only became desirable and realistic when European models of administration introduced new schemata, new ways of thinking about political power. These models showed how radically new institutions could be used to centralize power. Yet they could only be employed successfully because the king already had the resources with which to do it. If the king had lacked the authority to make law, to redefine institutions, to coerce provincial and local rulers, to levy taxes and raise armies, none of these European models would have been useful. Court officials, and local and provincial authorities, who lost the most in the reform process, would have rejected the program, as happened when similar reforms were introduced in Burma, China, and elsewhere.

In Siam, even more than in Japan, the structure of the conjunction was favorable. Elites in Siam—the king and his brothers—became interested in Western ideas before any dramatic losses compelled them to do so. There were no Opium Wars, loss of core territories, or bombardments of Siamese cities prior to the beginning of the reforms. These elites had substantial power already, due to the authority of the monarchy. Their primary obstacles were domestic: the assertion of effective control over the central government, and the training and financing of bureaucratic cadres to spread the new system.

In Siam, conceptual change was crucial in motivating reform. Material resources made it possible. Culture and power together created change.

Appendix I

Varieties of *Nai* and *Phrai*

A bewildering variety of different kinds of *phrai,* and therefore also of *nai,* existed under the old Thai manpower system. These varieties were often mutually overlapping and sometimes contradictory. The reader is therefore advised not to look for systematic logical coherence in this description; the categories were ad hoc, locally defined, and coined for administrative convenience.

Lek and *phrai* were interchangeable terms. One word or the other is conventionally used in certain contexts because it is considered more mellifluous, but that is the extent of the difference between them.

The major division among *phrai* was between royal *phrai* (*phrai luang*) and private *phrai* (*phrai som*). Much has been made of this division by Quaritch Wales, Akin, and others, but as Nuntiya points out, there was in practice little distinction between them outside of the capital.[1] Royal *phrai* were found throughout the kingdom, but outside of the capital they were referred to as *khong meuang,* meaning *phrai* of the *meuang.* They were under the control of the *cao meuang* and *kromakan,* who would also have private *phrai* of their own. In at least some *meuang* there were also *lek som khong meuang,* but it is not clear if these *som* were personal retainers of the officials who happened to be in the office of *cao meuang* or if they were actually attached to the office and changed hands when the office did.[2] Since there was relatively little supervision from the capital, and since tax collections and other matters passed through the *cao meuang* and his officials, in practice they could distribute work among their *phrai,* both private and royal, as they saw fit. Nuntiya seems to believe

---

[1] นันทิยา สว่างวุฒิธรรม, "การควบคุมกำลังคนในสมัยรัตนโกสินทร์ก่อนการจัดการเกณฑ์ทหาร (พศ ๒๓๒๕ - ๒๔๔๘)" [Nuntiya Swangvudthitham, "The Control of Manpower During the Bangkok Period Prior to the Introduction of Modern Conscription (BE 2325-2448)"] (MA Thesis in History, Chulalongkorn University, BE 2525), pp. 28, 32, 158; and อัญชลี สุสายัณห์, "ความเปลี่ยนแปลงของระบบไพร่และผลกระทบต่อสังคมไทยในรัชสมัยพระบาทสมเด็จพระจุลจอมเกล้า-เจ้าอยู่หัว" [Anchalee Susayanha, "Changes of the Phrai System and their Effects on Thai Society in the Reign of King Chulalongkorn"] (MA Thesis in History, Chulalongkorn University, BE 2524), p. 120. In practice probably the most germane distinction made between *phrai* was between *chakon* (able-bodied), *kae* or *phikan* (elderly or crippled), *ni* (fled), and *tai* (dead).

[2] ร. ๕ รล-กห ๗๐/๗๖, pp. 351-2; ป ๑๗/๔๒; รล-พศ ๓/๒๕๗.

that this led to a heavier burden for the royal *phrai* on the grounds that these officials would protect their private *phrai* more than *khong meuang*. Legally the royal *phrai* were also liable to a heavier tax burden. However, it should be observed that the royal *phrai* were actually in exactly the same position regarding the *cao* as other *phrai* were with any other *nai*. The *nai* was responsible for a tax assessment based on the number of *phrai* he had registered. This would make it a poor choice to overburden any one group, thereby driving them off. In fact, it seems much more likely that, since the tax assessments for royal *phrai* were higher, their *nai* would try his hardest either to embezzle them or convert them legally to private *phrai*. It is clear that the number of royal *phrai* declined over time.[3]

Lek khong meuang were usually responsible for *suai* and are hence often referred to as *phrai suai*. In the rolls such *phrai* are generally subdivided according to the specific goods they were supposed to supply, but the division seems to have had administrative uses as well since in many cases it persists even after most *phrai* were commuting their taxes to cash. Some royal *phrai* had other specialized jobs. Some who lived near the capital were registered to *Krom* Na (the Department of the Fields) and tended the king's private fields.[4] Others, called *lek dan* (border *lek*) patrolled border areas not only for the frontiers with other kingdoms but also between *meuang*.[5] There were also groups who cared for royal herds in the provinces, captured elephants, and so on. *Phrai* registered to the Royal Pages Corps would have been royal *phrai* but are often listed separately in the rolls.[6]

Another category of royal *phrai* included temple *phrai*. These were called *kha phra* (monk's servants) or *lek wat* (temple *lek*). They were tax-exempt *phrai* registered to temples, but their status was lower than that of regular *phrai luang* and shaded off into bondage. Some seem to have been personal servants of monks.

Private *phrai*, *lek som*, were sometimes personal retainers who might also be ordinary farmers. They had lower tax rates than royal *phrai*. The *lek som khong meuang*, for instance, would have been valuable to the officers of the *meuang* because they paid taxes at the rate of *som* rather than royal *phrai*.

Phrai were often identified by ethnic origin: Lao, Khmer, Vietnamese, and Malay *phrai* often appear on the rolls. Chinese who registered as *phrai* were referred to as a *cin phrai* – a Chinese who is a *phrai*.[7] In general, however, Chinese were not considered part of the *phrai* system. They paid different taxes and were administered in a different fashion. They needed to make a special effort to be registered as *phrai*. There were Siamese who tried to escape the *phrai* system by pretending to be Chinese. These were the *cin plaeng* – the "false Chinese" – who emulated Chinese

---

[3] See รล-พศ ๓/๗ ที่ ๔๐ ๑๒๔๖ ล. ๓ ร. ที่ ๖๓๖, pp. 59-61.

[4] นันทิยา, "การควบคุมกำลังคน" [Nuntiya , "Control of Manpower"], p. 18.

[5] Ibid., pp. 56-8.

[6] For instance in ร. ๕ บ ๑๗/๑.

[7] ร. ๕ รล-พศ ๓/๖๖, pp. 76-7. The grammar here is peculiar. Generally *phrai* who are identified ethnically are called *phrai*, with their ethnic origin added after as a modifier, e.g. *phrai lao* or *phrai khmen*. In this case, the person is referred to as Chinese, with *phrai* being used as the modifier, *cin phrai*. See also Kasian Tejapira, "Pigtail: A Pre-History of Chineseness in Siam," *Sojourn* 7,1 (1992): 108.

dress and wore the pigtail in order to do things forbidden to Siamese, most notably smoke opium.[8]

Phrai were also sometimes identified as *khoey su*, indicating that they or their ancestors had been captured in war. Some non-Thai *phrai* were referred to as *"asa,"* meaning literally "volunteers." According to King Chulalongkorn, these were private *phrai* who had been awarded to their *nai* as war captives or servants but who became royal *phrai* when their *nai* died.[9] These are to be distinguished from *chaloey*, war captives who were enslaved. These are differentiated in the rolls from ordinary *phrai* and from *that*, or debt bondsmen.[10]

Caophraya Mahinthaun, head of *Krom* Phrasurasawadi, claimed on the basis of chronicle sources that originally all *phrai* were royal *phrai*, but that after a long period of peace kings had gradually granted to various *nai* the privilege of holding private *phrai*, registering *phrai* in the Royal Pages corps, and making them tax-exempt in various ways. The result was that by the Fourth Reign *phrai* were increasingly slipping out of royal control.[11]

In fact there were a number of ways of getting out of *phrai* status. One could take a step down the social scale by selling oneself into slavery, becoming a *that*. On some of the rolls, we see the term *"lek that,"* presumably indicating someone born a *lek* who subsequently became a *that*, as distinct from the category of *"that"* alone, which must refer to people born into that condition.[12] Accepting *that* status earned one a lower tax burden, but it also bound one more closely to one's *nai*.

There were also a variety of tax-exempt statuses for relatives, personal servants, and close retainers of *nai* and nobles. The most basic was the *sip yok* or the *sip-ha yok*. For every ten or fifteen ordinary *phrai* a *munnai* registered, he could exempt one from

---

[8] Kasian, "Pigtail," p. 109.

[9] "พระราชดำรัสในพระบาทสมเด็จพระจุลจอมเกล้าเจ้าอยู่หัวทรงแถลงพระราชาธิบายแก้ไขการปกครอง แผ่นดิน" ["Proclamation of King Chulalongkorn Explaining the Improvements in the Administration of the Kingdom"] in ชัยอนันต์ สมุทวณิช และ ขัตติยา กรรณสูต รวบรวม, *เอกสาร การเมืองการปกครองไทย (พศ ๒๔๑๗ - ๒๔๗๗)* [Chai-anan Samudavanija and Khatthiya Kansut, eds., *Thai Political and Administrative Documents (BE 2417 - 2477)*] (Bangkok: Social Science Association of Thailand, BE 2532), pp. 93-4.

[10] As for instance in ร. ๔ บ ๑๗/๑๔. Sometimes, however, they are referred to as *chaloey pen that*, that is, war slaves who are bondsmen. The precise meaning of this formulation is not clear to me—it might suggest that some *chaloey* were closer to *phrai* status than *that*, or it might simply emphasize a distinction between *chaloey* and other kinds of *that*. See ร. ๔ บ ๑๗/๒๐. A distinction is sometimes made between *that* and *that som*, which seems to me to indicate that the former were originally *phrai luang*, while the former were originally *phrai som*. See ร. ๔ บ ๑๗/๔๓. This distinction does not seem to be made consistently, though. For that matter, a similar distinction is sometimes made between *chaloey* and *chaloey som*, as in ร. ๔ บ ๑๗/๑๖.

[11] ร. ๔ รล-พศ ๓/๔๐๖, pp. 445-9.

[12] These two categories sometimes occur on the same roll, indicating that there must be a difference between them. It seems to have been more difficult for those born as *that* to buy their freedom.

taxes.[13] Officials were also allowed a certain number of tax-exempt clerks and assistants according to their *sakdina*. These included *samian* and *thanai* (clerks), *samu banchi* (registrars), *baw* (servants), and *khunmeun*, who were sort of generic assistants. The position of *khunmeun* could also be purchased. In times of emergency, however, they might be corvéed along with ordinary *phrai*.

These tax-exempt assistants were gradually reduced in status to become the equivalent of a lower-level *nai*.[14] *Lek kaung nauk* — *phrai* residing outside of the capital, or outside a major *meuang*, but registered to a *nai* who lived within one of these places — were often controlled on a day-to-day basis by such low-level assistants as *khunmeun* or *samu banchi*. The terms *nai muat* and *nai kaung* were also basically interchangeable. The term *cao mu* is also sometimes used as a synonym, but since *mu* means generically any group, this term could be used as well to refer to higher-level officials. The term *cao nai* was also sometimes used, but this generally seems to refer to high level officials. *Kromakan* include a variety of offices, always at the local level, and *kromakan* could have a variety of titles and special functions.

The complexity of this system reflected the goals of the political order well: it provided lots of room for local conditions and lots of variety and flexibility of status, so that many different kinds of arrangements could be accommodated. No one was interested in creating uniformity or regularity; standardizing the system would only have made it harder to integrate people under a variety of circumstances. Allowing for flexibility provided much more leeway for negotiating the inclusion of as many people as possible in the political order, which was, after all, the goal of political practice.

---

[13] In practice the application of this rule seems to have been rather erratic. We frequently find cases of *munnai* with far too many or far too few *sip* or *sip-ha yok*. In ร. ๕ บ ๑๗/๑๓, for instance, a *nai* with fifty *phrai som* lists ten *sip yok* — twice as many as he should have — while in บ ๑๗/๔๘ a *nai* with eighty-three *phrai som*, four *that*, and thirty registered simply as *lek* (presumably being royal *phrai*) lists no *sip yok*, although he should have been entitled to ten of them.

[14] ปิยะฉัตร ปิตะวรรณ. *ระบบไพร่ในสังคมไทย พศ ๒๔๑๑-๒๔๕๓* [Piyachat Pitawan, *The Phrai System in Thai Society BE 2411-2453*] (Bangkok: Thammasat University Press, BE 2526), p. 12.

REIGN DATES OF KINGS MENTIONED IN THE TEXT

Thonburi Period:

King Taksin   1767-1782

Bangkok Period:

Rama I   1782-1809
Rama II   1809-1824
Rama III   1824-1851
Rama IV (King Mongkut)   1851-1868
Rama V (King Chulalongkorn)   1868-1910
Rama VI   1910-1925

BIBLIOGRAPHY

Archival Sources

In Thai:

Thai National Archives,
      4th Reign, Royal Secretariat-Ministry of the South (ร. 4 รล-กห),
      5th Reign, Ministry of Agriculture (ร. 5 กษ)
            Ministry of the North/Interior (ร. 5 ม)
            Ministry of the South/Defense (ร. 5 กห)
            Royal Secretariat (ร. 5 รล)
            Royal Secretariat-Ministry of the North (ร. 5 รล-มท)
            Royal Secretariat-Ministry of the South (ร. 5 รล-กห)
            Royal Secretariat-Special (ร. 5 รล-พศ)

Thai National Library, 4th Reign Documents (จดหมายเหตุ ร. 4)
                  Thesaphiban Journal (วารสาร เทศาภิบาล)
                  Wachirayan Journal (วชิรญาร)

In English:

Thai Khadi Research Institute, British Foreign Office Records (FO)

Works in Thai

กรมศิลปากร [Department of Fine Arts]. *กฎหมายตราสามดวง จ.ศ. ๑๑๖๖ (ประมวลกฎหมาย ร.*
    ๑) [*The Three Seals Law of C.S. 1166 (Law Code of Rama 1)*]. กรุงเทพฯ: กรมศิลป์,
    nd.

____. *จดหมายเหตุนครราชสีมา* [*Documents on Nakhon Ratchasima*]. กรุงเทพฯ: กรมศิลป์,
    2497.

____. *ประชุมพงศาวดาร ล. ๔๕, ๔๖* [*Collected Chronicles, vols. 45 and 46*]. กรุงเทพฯ:
    กรมศิลป์, พศ ๒๕๑๒.

คมเนตร ญาณโสภณ [Khomnet Yansophon]. อำนาจท้องถิ่นแบบจารีต และผลกระทบจากการ
เปลี่ยนแปลงการปกครองท้องถิ่นในยุคเทศาภิบาล [Traditional Local Power and the
Impact of the Change of Local Administration in the Thesaphiban Period].
วิทยานิพนธ์ คณะศิลปศาสตร์ มหาวิทยาลัยธรรมศาสตร์, พศ ๒๕๓๔.

ขจร สุขพานิช [Khachorn Sukhabhanij]. *ฐานันดรไพร่* [*The Status of Phrai*]. กรุงเทพฯ:
มหาวิทยาลัยศรีนครินทรวิโรฒ, พศ ๒๕๑๙.

ชัยอนันต์ สมุทวณิช และ ขัตติยา กรรณสูต รวบรวม [Chai-anan Samudavanija and Khatthiya
Kansut, eds]. *เอกสารการเมืองการปกครองไทย (พศ ๒๔๑๗ - ๒๔๗๗)* [*Thai Political
and Administrative Documents (BE 2417-2477)*]. กรุงเทพฯ: สมาคมสังคมศาสตร์แห่ง
ประเทศไทย, พศ ๒๕๓๒.

พระเจ้าน้องยาเธอ กรมหมื่น ไชยนาทเรนทร รวบรวม [Prince Chainatrenthon, ed.].
จดหมายเหตุเรื่องทัพเชียงตุง [*Documents on the Soldiers of Chiang Tung*]. อนุสรณ์
พระยานาวาพลพยุหรัษ, พศ ๒๔๕๙.

สมเด็จพระเจ้าบรมวงศ์เธอ กรมพระยาดำรงราชานุภาพ [Prince Damrong Rajanubhab]. *ความ
ทรงจำ* [*Memories*]. กรุงเทพฯ: สมาคมสังคม ศาสตร์แห่งประเทศไทย, พศ ๒๕๐๕.
_____. *เทศาภิบาล* [*Thesaphiban*]. กรุงเทพฯ: อนุสรณ์ พระยาอรรถกระวีสุนทร, พศ ๒๕๐๓.
_____. *นิทานโบราณคดี* [*Historical Tales*]. กรุงเทพฯ: คลังวิทยา, พศ ๒๕๑๗.
_____. *ลักษณะการปกครองประเทศสยามแต่โบราณ* [*Characteristics of Ancient Siamese
Government*]. กรุงเทพฯ: อนุสรณ์ ขูนสนิทประชากร, พศ ๒๕๒๔.

จักรกฤษณ์ นรนิติผดุงการ [Cakkrit Naranitiphadungkan]. *สมเด็จพระเจ้าบรมวงศ์เธอ
กรมพระยาดำรงราชานุภาพกับกระทรวงมหาดไทย* [*Prince Damrong Rachanubhab and
the Ministry of the Interior*]. กรุงเทพฯ: โอเดียนสโตร์, พศ ๒๕๒๗.

ณัฐวุฒิ สุทธิสงคราม [Natthawutthi Sutthisongkram]. *สมเด็จเจ้าพระยาบรมมหาศรีสุริยวงส์*
[*Somdet Caophraya Borommaha Si Suriyawong*]. กรุงเทพฯ: ศรีธรรม, พศ ๒๕๐๔.

เดช บุนนาค [Tej Bunnag]. *ขบถ รศ ๑๒๑* [*The Revolts of R.S. 121*]. กรุงเทพฯ: ไทยวัฒนาพานิช, พศ ๒๕๒๔.

ธีรชัย บุญมาธรรม [Theerachai Boonmathum]. ประวัติศาสตร์ท้องถิ่น ของหัวเมืองกาฬสินธุ์, พศ ๒๓๓๖-๒๔๕๐ [A Local History of Huamuang Kalasin, 1793-1907"]. วิทยานิพนธ์ภาควิชา ประวัติศาสตร์ จุฬาลงกรณ์มหาวิทยาลัย, พศ ๒๕๒๘.

นงลักษณ์ ลิ้มศิริ [Nonglak Limsiri]. ความสำคัญของกบฏหัวเมืองอีสาน พศ ๒๓๒๕-๒๔๔๕ [The Significance of the Rebellions in the Northeastern Provinces of Thailand, BE 2325 – 2445]. วิทยานิพนธ์ ภาควิชาประวัติศาสตร์ จุฬาลงกรณ์มหาวิทยาลัย, พศ ๒๕๒๔.

นันทิยา สว่างวุฒิธรรม [Nuntiya Swangvudthitham]. การควบคุมกำลัง คนในสมัยรัตนโกสินทร์ ก่อนการจัดการเกณฑ์ทหาร (พศ ๒๓๒๕-๒๔๔๘) [The Control of Manpower During the Bangkok Period Prior to the Introduction of Modern Conscription (BE 2325-2448)]. วิทยานิพนธ์ ภาควิชาประวัติศาสตร์ จุฬาลงกรณ์ มหาวิทยาลัย, พศ ๒๕๒๕.

นิติ กสิโกศล [Niti Kasikoson]. การเก็บค่านาในสมัยกรุงรัตนโกสินทร์ พศ ๒๓๒๕-๒๔๘๒ [The Collection of Kha-na (Rice-land Tax) In the Early Bangkok Period 1782-1939]. วิทยานพินธ์ สาขาวิชาประวัติศาสตร์ เอเชียตะวันออกเฉียงใต้มหาวิทยาลัย ศิลปากร, พศ ๒๕๒๕.

นิธิ เอียวศรีวงศ์ [Nithi Aeusrivongse]. *ปากไก่และใบเรือ* [*Quill and Sail*]. กรุงเทพฯ: อมรินทร์การพิมพ์, พศ ๒๕๒๗.

_____. *ลัทธิพิธีเสด็จพ่อ ร. ๕* [*The Cult of Royal Father Rama V*]. กรุงเทพฯ: ศิลปวัฒนธรรม, พศ ๒๕๓๖.

บุญรอด แก้วกันหา [Boonrod Keawkanha]. การเก็บส่วยในสมัย รัตนโกสินทร์ตอนต้น (พศ ๒๓๒๕ - ๒๔๑๑) [The Collection of Suay During the Early Ratanakosin Period (AD 1782-1868)]. วิทยานิพนธ์ ภาควิชาประวัติศาสตร์ จุฬาลงกรณ์มหาวิทยาลัย, พศ ๒๕๑๘.

หมอ ปรัดเล [D.B. Bradley, ed.]. *หนังสืออักขราภิธานศรับท์* [*Dictionary of the Siamese Language*]. กรุงเทพฯ: คุรุสภา, พศ ๒๕๑๔ [๒๔๖].

ปิยะฉัตร ปิตวรรณ [Piyachat Pitawan]. *ระบบไพร่ในสังคมไทย พศ ๒๔๑๑-๒๔๕๓* [*The Phrai System in Thai Society BE 2411-2453*]. กรุงเทพฯ: มหาวิทยาลัยธรรมศาสตร์, พศ ๒๕๒๖.

ประภาส จารุเสถียร รวบรวม [Praphat Carusathian, ed]. *ประชุมประกาศรัชกาลที่ ๔* [*Collected Proclamations of the Fourth Reign*]. อนุสรณ์ พระมหาโพธิวงศาจารย์ อินทโชตเถระ, พศ ๒๕๑๑.

วุฒิชัย มูลศิลป์ [Wutichai Munsin]. *การปฏิรูปการศึกษาในสมัย พระบาทสมเด็จ พระจุลจอมเกล้าเจ้าอยู่หัว* [*The Reformation of Education in the Reign of King Chulalongkorn*]. กรุงเทพฯ: ไทยวัฒนาพานิช, พศ ๒๕๒๙.

สภาลินี ขมะสุนทร [Suphalini Khamasunthon]. แนวความคิดทางการเมืองของกลุ่มผู้นำในรัช-สมัยพระบาทสมเด็จพระจุลจอมเกล้าเจ้าอยู่หัวระหว่าง พศ ๒๕๐๐-๒๔๓๖ [*The Political Thoughts of Elite Groups During the Reign of King Chulalongkorn BE 2400 - 2436*]. วิทยานิพนธ์ ภาควิชาประวัติศาสตร์ จุฬาลงกณ์มหาวิทยาลัย, พศ ๒๕๒๙.

สุมาลี บำรุงสุข [Sumalee Bumroongsook]. การรวบรวมรายได้แผ่นดิน ในรัชกาลพระบาทสมเด็จ-พระจุลจอมเกล้าเจ้าอยู่หัว (พศ ๒๔๑๖ - ๒๔๕๓) [*The Consolidation of Government Revenue in the Reign of King Chulalongkorn (1873 - 1910)*]. วิทยานิพนธ์ ภาค วิชาประวัติศาสตร์ จุฬาลงกรณ์มหาวิทยาลัย, พศ ๒๕๒๕.

เจ้าพระยาสุรศักมนตรี [*Caophraya* Surasakamontri]. *ประวัติการของเจ้าพระยาสุรศักมนตรี, ๔ เล่ม* [*The Life of Caophraya Surasakamontri, 4 vols.*]. กรุงเทพฯ: ศึกสาภัณฑ์พานิชย์, พศ ๒๕๐๔.

เสถียร ลายลักษณ์ และคนอื่นๆ รวบรวม [Sathian Laialak et. al., eds]. *ประชุมกฎหมายประจำศก* [*Collected Laws*]. กรุงเทพฯ: โรงพิมพ์เดลิเมลล์, พศ ๒๔๗๘.

อริยา เสถียรสุต [Ariya Sathiansut]. เจ้าเมืองนครศรีธรรมราชสมัยการปกครองแบบเก่าแห่งกรุง
รัตนโกสินทร์ [The Governorship of Ligor Under the Old System of Government of the Bangkok Period]. วิทยานิพนธ์ ภาควิชาประวัติศาสตร์ จุฬาลงกรณ์มหาวิท-
ยาลัย, พศ ๒๕๑๔.

อัญชลี สุสายัณห์ [Anchalee Susayanha]. ความเปลี่ยนแปลงของระบบไพร่และผลกระทบต่อสัง-
คมไทยในรัชสมัยพระบาทสมเด็จพระจุลจอมเกล้าเจ้าอยู่หัว [Changes of the Phrai System and Their Effects on Thai Society in the Reign of King Chulalongkorn].
วิทยานิพนธ์ ภาควิชาประวัติศาสตร์ จุฬาลงกรณ์มหาวิทยาลัย, พศ ๒๕๒๔.

อำมาตย์โท พระยาสากลกิจประมวญ, รวบรวม [Amattho Phraya Sakonkitpramuan, ed.].
ประชุมจดหมายเหตุเรื่องปราบกบฏเวียงจันท์ [Collected Documents on Suppressing the
Wiang Chan Rebellion]. อนุสรณ์ เจ้าจอมมารดา ม.ร.ว. แสง, พศ ๒๕๗๓.

Works in English

Adas, Michael. *The Burma Delta: Economic Development and Social Change on an Asian
Rice Frontier, 1852-1941*. Madison: University of Wisconsin Press, 1974.

_____. "From Avoidance to Confrontation: Peasant Protest in Precolonial and
Colonial Southeast Asia." *Comparative Studies in Society and History* 23:2
(April 1981).

_____. "Bandits, Monks and Pretender Kings: Patterns of Peasant Resistance and
Protest in Colonial Burma, 1826-1941." In *Power and Protest in the Countryside:
Rural Unrest in Asia, Europe, and Latin America*. Ed. Robert P. Weller and Scott
E. Guggenheim. Durham: Duke University Press, 1989.

Akin Rabibhadana. *The Organization of Thai Society in the Early Bangkok Period, 1782-
1873*. Ithaca: Cornell University Southeast Asia Program, 1969.

Anderson, Benedict. "The Idea of Power in Javanese Culture." In *Language and Power:
Exploring Political Cultures in Indonesia*. Ithaca: Cornell University Press, 1990.

Anonymous (James McCarthy). *An Englishman's Siamese Journals, 1890-1893*.
Bangkok: Siam Media International, no date (1895).

Aung-Thwin, Michael. "Hierarchy and Order in Pre-Colonial Burma." *Journal of
Southeast Asian Studies* 15:2 (September 1984).

_____. *Irrigation in the Heartland of Burma: Foundations of the Pre-Colonial Burmese
State*. DeKalb: Northern Illinois University Center for South and Southeast
Asian Studies Occasional Paper #15, 1990.

Batson, Benjamin. *Siam's Political Future: Documents from the End of the Absolute Monarchy*. Ithaca: Cornell Southeast Asian Studies Program Data Paper #96, 1974.

Battye, Noel Alfred. "The Military, Government and Society in Siam, 1868-1910: Politics and Military Reform During the Reign of King Chulalongkorn." PhD Dissertation, Cornell University, 1974.

Bechstedt, Hans-Dieter. "Identity and Authority in Thailand." In *National Identity and its Defenders: Thailand, 1939-1989*, ed. Craig J. Reynolds. Chiang Mai: Silkworm Books, 1991.

Bendix, Reinhard. *Kings or People: Power and the Mandate to Rule*. Berkeley: University of California, 1978.

Benedict, Ruth. *The Chrysanthemum and the Sword: Patterns of Japanese Culture*. New York: Houghton Mifflin, 1946.

Bennett, Paul J. *Conference Under the Tamarind Tree: Three Essays in Burmese History*. New Haven: Yale Southeast Asia Series #15, 1971.

Bourdieu, Pierre. *Outline of a Theory of Practice*, trans. Richard Nice. New York: Cambridge University Press, 1977.

Bowie, Katherine Ann. "Peasant Perspectives on the Political Economy of the Northern Thai Kingdom of Chiang Mai in the Nineteenth Century." PhD Dissertation, University of Chicago, 1988.

Bowring, Sir John. *The Kingdom and People of Siam*, 2 vols. New York: Oxford University Press, 1969 (1857).

Brailey, Nigel. "The Origins of the Siamese Forward Movement in Western Laos: 1850-92." PhD Dissertation, University of London, 1968.

Breazeale, Kennon. "The Integration of the Lao States into the Thai Kingdom." PhD Dissertation, Oxford University, 1975.

Brown, Ian. *The Elite and the Economy in Siam, c. 1890-1920*. Singapore: Oxford University Press, 1988.

Bunnag, Jane. *Buddhist Monk, Buddhist Layman: A Study of Urban Monastic Organization in Central Thailand*. New York: Cambridge University Press, 1973.

Cady, John F. *A History of Modern Burma*. Ithaca: Cornell University Press, 1958.

Calavan, Sharon Kay Mitchell. "Aristocrats and Commoners in Rural Northern Thailand." PhD Dissertation, University of Illinois at Champagne-Urbana, 1974.

Chamberlain, James, ed. *The Ram Khamhaeng Controversy: Collected Papers*. Bangkok: Siam Society, 1991.

Chatchai Panananon. "Siamese 'Slavery': The Institution and its Abolition." PhD Dissertation, University of Michigan, 1982.

Chatthip Nartsupha. "The Ideology of Holy Men Revolts in North East Thailand." In *History and Peasant Consciousness in Southeast Asia*, ed. Andrew Turton and Shigeharu Tanabe. Osaka: National Museum of Ethnography, 1984.

Chatthip Nartsupha and Suthy Prasartset, eds. *Political Economy of Siam, 1851-1910*. Bangkok: Social Science Association of Thailand, 1978.

Chula Chakrabongse. *Lords of Life: A History of the Kings of Thailand*. London: Redman, 1967.

Crawfurd, John. *The Crawfurd Papers*. Bangkok: Vajiranana National Library, 1915.

Cushman, Jennifer. *Family and State: The Formation of a Sino-Thai Tin-Mining Dynasty, 1797-1932*. New York: Oxford University Press, 1991.
____. *Fields from the Sea: Chinese Junk Trade with Siam During the Late Eighteenth and Early Nineteenth Centuries*. Ithaca: Cornell Southeast Asia Program Publications, 1993.

D'Andrade, Roy. *The Development of Cognitive Anthropology*. New York: Cambridge University Press, 1995.

D'Andrade, Roy and Claudia Strauss, eds. *Human Motives and Cultural Models*. New York: Cambridge University Press, 1992.

Prince Dhani. "The Old Siamese Conception of the Monarchy." *Journal of the Siam Society* 36,2 (1947).

Donner, Wolf. *The Five Faces of Thailand: An Economic Geography*. St. Lucia, Queensland: Queensland University Press, 1982.

Dore, Ronald. *Education in Tokugawa Japan*. Berkeley: University of California Press, 1965.

Engel, David. *Law and Kingship in Thailand During the Reign of King Chulalongkorn*. Ann Arbor: University of Michigan Center for South and Southeast Asian Studies Paper #9, 1975.
____. *Code and Custom in a Thai Provincial Court: the Interaction of Formal and Informal Systems of Justice*. Tucson: University of Arizona Press, 1978.

Englehart, Neil A. "Culture, Choice and Change in Thailand in the Reign of King Chulalongkorn, 1868-1910." PhD Dissertation, University of California, San Diego, 1996.

Feeny, David. "The Decline of Property Rights in Man in Thailand 1800-1913." *Journal of Economic History* 49:2 (June 1989).

Furnivall, J. S. *Colonial Policy and Practice: A Comparative Study of Burma and Netherlands India*. London: Cambridge University Press, 1948.

Geertz, Clifford. *Negara: The Theatre State in Nineteenth-Century Bali*. Princeton: Princeton University Press, 1980.

Gesick, Lorraine. "Kingship and Political Integration in Traditional Siam, 1767-1824." PhD Dissertation, Cornell University, 1976.

Hallet, Holt. *A Thousand Miles on An Elephant in the Shan States*. London: William Blackwood & Sons, 1890.

Hanks, Lucien. *Rice and Man: Agricultural Ecology in Southeast Asia*. Chicago: Aldive-Atherton, 1972.
_____. "The Thai Social Order as Entourage and Circle." In *Change and Persistence in Thai Society: Essays in Honor of Lauriston Sharp*, ed. G. William Skinner and A. Thomas Kirsch. Ithaca: Cornell University Press, 1975.
_____. "Merit and Power in the Thai Social Order." In *Modern Thai Politics: From Village to Nation*, ed. Clark Neher. Cambridge, MA: Schenkman, 1976.

Hegel, G. W. F. *Phenomenology of Spirit*, trans. A. V. Miller. New York: Oxford University Press, 1977.

Hintze, Otto. *The Historical Essays of Otto Hintze*, ed. Felix Gilbert. New York: Oxford University Press, 1975.

Hobsbawm, Eric. *Bandits*, revised edition. New York: Pantheon, 1981.

Hong Lysa. "The Tax-Farming System in the Early Bangkok Period." *Journal of Southeast Asian Studies* 14,2 (1983).
_____. *Thailand in the Nineteenth Century: Evolution of Economy and Society*. Singapore: Institute of Southeast Asian Studies, 1984.

House, Samuel. "History of the Missions in Siam and Laos." In *Siam and Laos as Seen By Our American Missionaries*. Philadelphia: Presbyterian Board of Publications, 1884.

Inden, Ronald. *Imagining India*. New York: Basil Blackwell, 1990.

Ingersoll, Joseph. "Merit and Identity in Village Thailand." In *Change and Persistence in Thai Society: Essays in Honor of Lauriston Sharp*, ed. G. William Skinner and A. Thomas Kirsch. Ithaca: Cornell University Press, 1975.

Ingram, James C. *Economic Change in Thailand, 1850-1970*. Stanford: Stanford University Press, 1971.

Ishii, Yoneo. *Sangha, State and Society: Thai Buddhism in History*, trans. Peter Hawkes. Honolulu: University of Hawai'i Press, 1986.

Jeshurun, Chandran. *Contest for Siam 1889-1902: A Study in Diplomatic Rivalry*. Kuala Lumpur: Penerbit Universiti Kebangsaan Malaysia, 1977.

Johnston, David Bruce. "Rural Society and the Rice Economy in Thailand, 1880-1930." PhD Dissertation, Yale University, 1975.
____. "Bandit, *Nakleng* and Peasant in Rural Thai Society." *Contributions to Asian Studies* 15 (1980).

Kamala Tiyavanich. *Forest Recollections: Wandering Monks in Twentieth Century Thailand*. Honolulu: University of Hawai'i Press, 1997.

Kasian Tejapira. "Pigtail: A Pre-History of Chineseness in Siam." *Sojourn* 7,1 (1992).

Keeton, Charles Lee. *King Thebaw and the Ecological Rape of Burma: The Political and Commercial Struggle Between British India and French Indo-China in Burma, 1878-1886*. Delhi: Manohar Book Service, 1974.

Kemp, Jeremy. "The Manipulation of Personal Relationships: From Kinship to Patron-Clientage." In *Strategies and Structures in Thai Society*, ed. Hans ten Brummelhuis and Jeremy Kemp. Amsterdam: Anthropologisch-Sociologisch, Universiteit van Amsterdam, #31 Publikatieserie Vakgroep Zuid-en Zuidoest-Azie, 1984.

Keyes, Charles. "Millenarianism, Theravada Buddhism and Thai Society." *Journal of Asian Studies* 36,2 (1977).

Kirsch, A. Thomas. "Modernizing Implications of Nineteenth-Century Reforms in the Thai Sangha." In *Religion and the Legitimation of Power in Thailand, Laos and Burma*, ed. Bardwell Smith. Chambersberg, PA: Anima, 1978.

Klausner, William J. *Reflections on Thai Culture: Collected Writings of William J. Klausner*. Bangkok: Siam Society, 1993.

Koenig, William J. *The Burmese Polity 1752-1819: Politics, Administration and Social Organization in the Early Kon-baung Period*. Ann Arbor: Michigan Papers on South and Southeast Asia #34, 1990.

Koizumi, Junko. "The Commutation of *Suai* from Northeast Thailand in the Middle of the Nineteenth Century." *Journal of Southeast Asian Studies* 23,2 (1992).

Levi, Margaret. *Of Rule and Revenue*. Berkeley: University of California Press, 1988.

Ma Kyan. "King Mindon's Councillors." *Journal of the Burma Research Society* 44:1 (June 1961).

Magagna, Victor V. *Communities of Grain: Rural Rebellion in Comparative Perspective.* Ithaca: Cornell University Press, 1991.

Mayoury Ngaosyvathn and Pheuiphanh Ngaosyvathn. *Paths to Conflagration: Fifty Years of Diplomacy and Warfare in Laos, Thailand and Vietnam, 1778-1828.* Ithaca: Cornell Southeast Asia Program, 1998.

McCarthy, James. *Surveying and Exploring in Siam.* London: John Murray, 1900.

Metzger, Thomas. *Escape from Predicament: Neo-Confucianism and China's Evolving Political Culture.* New York: Columbia University Press, 1977.

Moore, Barrington. *The Social Origins of Dictatorship and Democracy: Lord and Peasant in the Making of the Modern World.* Boston: Beacon Press, 1966.

Murdoch, John B. "1901-2 'Holy Man's Rebellion'." *Journal of the Siam Society* 62,1 (1974).

Myo Myint. "The Politics of Survival in Burma: Diplomacy and Statecraft in the Reign of King Mindon, 1853-1878." PhD Dissertation, Cornell University, 1987.

Nash, Manning. *The Golden Road to Modernity: Village Life in Contemporary Burma.* New York: John Wiley, 1965.

Olson, Mancur. *The Logic of Collective Action: Public Goods and the Theory of Groups.* Cambridge, MA: Harvard University Press, 1965.

Pallegoix, D. J. B. สัพพะจะนะ พาสาไทย / *Dictionarium Linguae Thai Sive Siamensis.* Paris: Jussu Imperatoris Impressum, 1854.

Pollak, Oliver. *Empires in Collision: Anglo-Burmese Relations in the Mid-Nineteenth Century.* Westport: Greenwood Press, 1979.

Potter, Jack. *Thai Peasant Social Structure.* Chicago: University of Chicago Press, 1976.

Ramsay, James Ansil. "The Development of a Bureaucratic Polity: The Case of Northern Siam." PhD Dissertation, Cornell University, 1971.
_____. "Modernization and Reactionary Rebellions in Northern Siam." *Journal of Asian Studies* 38,2 (1979).

Reynolds, Craig J. "The Buddhist Monkhood in Nineteenth-Century Thailand." PhD Dissertation, Cornell University, 1972.
_____. "Feudalism as a Trope or Discourse for the Asian Past with Special Reference to Thailand." In Edmund Leach, S. N. Murkherjee and John Ward, eds.,

Feudalism: Comparative Studies. Sydney: Sydney Studies in Society and Culture, 1985.

____. *Thai Radical Discourse: The Real Face of Thai Feudalism Today.* Ithaca: Cornell Southeast Asia Program, 1987.

Reynolds, Frank E. and Mani B., trans. *The Three Worlds According to King Ruang: A Thai Buddhist Cosmology.* Berkeley: University of California Press, 1982.

M. R. W. Rujaya Abhakorn. "Ratburi, An Inner Province: Local Government and Central Politics in Siam, 1862-1892." PhD Dissertation, Cornell University, 1984.

Rhys Davids, C. A. F. and T. W., trans. *Dialogues of the Buddha,* part III. London: Pali Text Society, 1965.

Rhys Davids, T. W., trans. *The Questions of King Milinda,* 2 volumes. Delhi: Motital Banarsidass, 1975 [1890].

Sahlins, Marshall. *Islands of History.* Chicago: University of Chicago Press, 1985.

Sarasin Viraphol. *Tribute and Profit: Sino-Siamese Trade, 1652-1853.* Cambridge, MA: Harvard University Press, 1977.

Scott, James. *Moral Economy of the Peasant: Rebellion and Resistance in Southeast Asia.* New Haven: Yale University Press, 1976.

M. R. W. Seni and M. R. W. Kukrit Promoj, *A King of Siam Speaks.* Bangkok: Siam Society, 1987.

Sharp, Lauriston and Lucien M. Hanks. *Bang Chan: Social History of a Rural Community in Thailand.* Ithaca: Cornell University Press, 1978.

Siffin, William J. *The Thai Bureaucracy: Institutional Change and Development.* Honolulu: East-West Center, 1966.

Skinner, G. William. *Chinese Society in Thailand: An Analytical History.* Ithaca: Cornell University Press, 1957.

Skocpol, Theda. *States and Social Revolutions: A Comparative Analysis of France, Russia, and China.* New York: Cambridge University Press, 1979.

Smith, Thomas. *The Agrarian Origins of Modern Japan.* Stanford: Stanford University Press, 1959.

____. *Native Sources of Japanese Industrialization, 1750-1920.* Berkeley: University of California Press, 1988.

Snit Snuckarn and Kennon Breazeale. *A Culture in Search of Survival: The Phuan of Thailand and Laos.* New Haven: Yale Southeast Asian Studies, 1988.

Somboon Suksamran. *Political Patronage and Control Over the Sangha.* Singapore: Institute of Southeast Asian Studies Research Notes and Discussion Papers #28, 1981.

Sompop Manarungsan. *Economic Development of Thailand, 1850-1950: Response to the Challenge of the World Economy.* Bangkok: Chulalongkorn University Institute of Asian Studies, 1989.

Sternstein, Larry. "The Distribution of Thai Centres at Mid-Nineteenth Century." *Journal of Southeast Asian History* 7,1 (1966).

Strauss, Claudia and Naomi Quinn. *A Cognitive Theory of Cultural Meaning.* New York: Cambridge University Press, 1997.

Strong, John. *The Legend of King Asoka: A Study and Translation of the Asokavadana.* Princeton: Princeton University Press, 1983.

Tambiah, Stanley. *Buddhism and the Spirit Cults in North-east Thailand.* New York: Cambridge University Press, 1970.
_____. *World Conqueror and World Renouncer: A Study of Buddhism and Polity in Thailand Against a Historical Background.* New York: Cambridge University Press, 1976.
_____. *Buddhist Saints of the Forest and the Cult of Amulets: A Study of Charisma, Hagiography, Sectarianism, and Millennial Buddhism.* New York: Cambridge University Press, 1984.

Tannenbaum, Nicola. *Who Can Compete Against the World? Power-Protection and Buddhism in Shan Worldview.* Ann Arbor: Association for Asian Studies, 1995.

Tej Bunnag. *The Provincial Administration of Siam, 1892-1915: The Ministry of the Interior under Prince Damrong Rajanubhab.* New York: Oxford University Press, 1977.

Terwiel, B. J. *Monks and Magic: An Analysis of Religious Ceremonies in Central Thailand.* Lund: Scandinavian Institute of Asian Studies, 1975.
_____. "Tattooing in Thailand's History." In *Journal of the Royal Asiatic Society* #2, 1979.
_____. *Through Traveller's Eyes: An Approach to Nineteenth-Century Thai History.* Bangkok: Duang Komol, 1989.

Thongchai Winichakul. *Siam Mapped: A History of the Geo-Body of a Nation.* Honolulu: University of Hawai'i, 1994.

Tilly, Charles, ed. *The Formation of National States in Western Europe.* Princeton: Princeton University Press, 1975.

Tilly, Charles. *Coercion, Capital and European States, AD 990-1990.* Cambridge: Basil Blackwell, 1990.

Trager, Frank and William J. Koenig with Yi Yi. *Burmese Sit-tans 1764-1826: Records of Rural Life and Administration.* Tuscon: University of Arizona Press, 1979.

Turton, Andrew. "Thai Institutions of Slavery." In *Asian and African Systems of Slavery*, ed. James Watson. Berkeley: University of California Press, 1980.

Vickery, Michael. "Thai Regional Elites and the Reforms of King Chulalongkorn." *Journal of Asian Studies* 29,4 (1970).

van der Heide, J. Homan. "The Economical Development of Siam During the Last Half-Century." *Journal of the Siam Society* 3,2 (1906).

Vella, Walter. *Impact of the West on Government in Thailand.* Berkeley: University of California Press, 1955.
____. *Siam Under Rama III, 1824-1851.* Locust Valley, New York: J. J. Augustin, 1957.

Wales, H. G. Quaritch. *Siamese State Ceremonies: Their History and Function.* London: Bernard Quaritch, 1931.
____. *Ancient Siamese Government and Administration.* New York: Paragon, 1965.

Weber, Max. *Economy and Society*, 2 vols. Guenther Roth and Claus Wittich, eds. Berkeley: University of California Press, 1978.
____. *The Methodology of the Social Sciences.* Edward Shils and Henry Finch, trans. and ed. New York: Free Press, 1949.
____. *The Protestant Ethic and the Spirit of Capitalism*, trans. Talcott Parson. New York: Scribner, 1930.

Westney, D. Eleanor. *Imitation and Innovation: The Transfer of Western Organizational Patterns to Meiji Japan.* Cambridge, MA: Harvard University Press, 1987.

Wijeyewardene, Gehan. "The Frontiers of Thailand." In *National Identity and Its Defenders: Thailand 1939-1989*, ed. Craig J. Reynolds. Chiang Mai: Silkworm Books, 1991.

Wilson, Constance. "State and Society in the Reign of King Mongkut, 1851-1868: Thailand on the eve of Modernization." PhD Dissertation, Cornell University, 1970.
____. "The *Nai Kong* in Thai Administration, 1824-68." *Contributions to Asian Studies* 15 (1980).
____. "The Holy Man in the History of Thailand and Laos." *Journal of Southeast Asian Studies* 28,2 (1997).

Wyatt, David. "Siam and Laos, 1767-1827." *Journal of Southeast Asian History* 4,2 (1963).
____. "Family Politics in Nineteenth Century Thailand." *Journal of Southeast Asian History* 9,2 (1968).
____. *The Politics of Reform in Thailand: Education in the Reign of King Chulalongkorn.* New Haven: Yale University Press, 1969.

____. "Education and the Modernization of Thai Society." In *Change and Persistence in Thai Society: Essays in Honor of Lauriston Sharp*, ed. G. William Skinner and A. Thomas Kirsch. Ithaca: Cornell University Press, 1975.

____. *Thailand: A Short History*. New Haven: Yale University Press, 1982.

Xie Shunyu, *Siam and the British, 1874-5: Sir Andrew Clarke and the Front Palace Crisis*. Bangkok: Thammasat University Press, 1988.

SOUTHEAST ASIA PROGRAM PUBLICATIONS
Cornell University

Studies on Southeast Asia

Number 29   *Studies in Southeast Asian Art: Essays in Honor of Stanley J. O'Connor,* ed. Nora A. Taylor. 2000. 243 pp. Illustrations. ISBN 0-87727-728-1

Number 28   *The Hadrami Awakening: Community and Identity in the Netherlands East Indies, 1900-1942,* Natalie Mobini-Kesheh. 1999. 174 pp. ISBN 0-87727-727-3

Number 27   *Tales from Djakarta: Caricatures of Circumstances and their Human Beings,* Pramoedya Ananta Toer. 1999. 145 pp. ISBN 0-87727-726-5

Number 26   *History, Culture, and Region in Southeast Asian Perspectives,* rev. ed., O. W. Wolters. 1999. 275 pp. ISBN 0-87727-725-7

Number 25   *Figures of Criminality in Indonesia, the Philippines, and Colonial Vietnam,* ed. Vicente L. Rafael. 1999. 259 pp. ISBN 0-87727-724-9

Number 24   *Paths to Conflagration: Fifty Years of Diplomacy and Warfare in Laos, Thailand, and Vietnam, 1778-1828,* Mayoury Ngaosyvathn and Pheuiphanh Ngaosyvathn. 1998. 268 pp. ISBN 0-87727-723-0

Number 23   *Nguyễn Cochinchina: Southern Vietnam in the Seventeenth and Eighteenth Centuriess,* Li Tana. 1998. 194 pp. ISBN 0-87727-722-2

Number 22   *Young Heroes: The Indonesian Family in Politics,* Saya S. Shiraishi. 1997. 183 pp. ISBN 0-87727-721-4

Number 21   *Interpreting Development: Capitalism, Democracy, and the Middle Class in Thailand,* John Girling. 1996. 95 pp. ISBN 0-87727-720-6

Number 20   *Making Indonesia,* ed. Daniel S. Lev, Ruth McVey. 1996. 201 pp. ISBN 0-87727-719-2

Number 19   *Essays into Vietnamese Pasts,* ed. K. W. Taylor, John K. Whitmore. 1995. 288 pp. ISBN 0-87727-718-4

Number 18   *In the Land of Lady White Blood: Southern Thailand and the Meaning of History,* Lorraine M. Gesick. 1995. 106 pp. ISBN 0-87727-717-6

Number 17   *The Vernacular Press and the Emergence of Modern Indonesian Consciousness,* Ahmat Adam. 1995. 220 pp. ISBN 0-87727-716-8

Number 16   *The Nan Chronicle,* trans., ed. David K. Wyatt. 1994. 158 pp. ISBN 0-87727-715-X

Number 15   *Selective Judicial Competence: The Cirebon-Priangan Legal Administration, 1680–1792,* Mason C. Hoadley. 1994. 185 pp. ISBN 0-87727-714-1

Number 14   *Sjahrir: Politics and Exile in Indonesia,* Rudolf Mrázek. 1994. 536 pp. ISBN 0-87727-713-3

Number 13   *Fair Land Sarawak: Some Recollections of an Expatriate Officer,* Alastair Morrison. 1993. 196 pp. ISBN 0-87727-712-5

Number 12   *Fields from the Sea: Chinese Junk Trade with Siam during the Late Eighteenth and Early Nineteenth Centuries,* Jennifer Cushman. 1993. 206 pp. ISBN 0-87727-711-7

Number 11   *Money, Markets, and Trade in Early Southeast Asia: The Development of Indigenous Monetary Systems to AD 1400,* Robert S. Wicks. 1992. 2nd printing 1996. 354 pp., 78 tables, illus., maps. ISBN 0-87727-710-9

Number 10   *Tai Ahoms and the Stars: Three Ritual Texts to Ward Off Danger*, trans., ed. B. J. Terwiel, Ranoo Wichasin. 1992. 170 pp. ISBN 0-87727-709-5

Number 9   *Southeast Asian Capitalists,* ed. Ruth McVey. 1992. 2nd printing 1993. 220 pp. ISBN 0-87727-708-7

Number 8   *The Politics of Colonial Exploitation: Java, the Dutch, and the Cultivation System*, Cornelis Fasseur, ed. R. E. Elson, trans. R. E. Elson, Ary Kraal. 1992. 2nd printing 1994. 266 pp. ISBN 0-87727-707-9

Number 7   *A Malay Frontier: Unity and Duality in a Sumatran Kingdom*, Jane Drakard. 1990. 215 pp. ISBN 0-87727-706-0

Number 6   *Trends in Khmer Art*, Jean Boisselier, ed. Natasha Eilenberg, trans. Natasha Eilenberg, Melvin Elliott. 1989. 124 pp., 24 plates. ISBN 0-87727-705-2

Number 5   *Southeast Asian Ephemeris: Solar and Planetary Positions, A.D. 638–2000*, J. C. Eade. 1989. 175 pp. ISBN 0-87727-704-4

Number 3   *Thai Radical Discourse: The Real Face of Thai Feudalism Today*, Craig J. Reynolds. 1987. 2nd printing 1994. 186 pp. ISBN 0-87727-702-8

Number 1   *The Symbolism of the Stupa*, Adrian Snodgrass. 1985. Revised with index, 1988. 3rd printing 1998. 469 pp. ISBN 0-87727-700-1

SEAP Series

Number 18   *Culture and Power in Traditional Siamese Government*, Neil A. Englehart. 2000. 130 pp. ISBN 0-87727-135-6

Number 17   *Gangsters, Democracy, and the State*, ed. Carl A. Trocki. 1998. 94 pp. ISBN 0-87727-134-8

Number 16   *Cutting Across the Lands: An Annotated Bibliography on Natural Resource Management and Community Development in Indonesia, the Philippines, and Malaysia*, ed. Eveline Ferretti. 1997. 329 pp. ISBN 0-87727-133-X

Number 15   *The Revolution Falters: The Left in Philippine Politics After 1986*, ed. Patricio N. Abinales. 1996. 182 pp. ISBN 0-87727-132-1

Number 14   *Being Kammu: My Village, My Life*, ed. Damrong Tayanin. 1994. 138 pp., 22 tables, illus., maps. ISBN 0-87727-130-5

Number 13   *The American War in Vietnam*, ed. Jayne Werner, David Hunt. 1993. 132 pp. ISBN 0-87727-131-3

Number 12   *The Political Legacy of Aung San*, ed. Josef Silverstein. Revised edition 1993. 169 pp. ISBN 0-87727-128-3

Number 10   *Studies on Vietnamese Language and Literature: A Preliminary Bibliography*, Nguyen Dinh Tham. 1992. 227 pp. ISBN 0-87727-127-5

Number 9   *A Secret Past*, Dokmaisot, trans. Ted Strehlow. 1992. 2nd printing 1997. 72 pp. ISBN 0-87727-126-7

Number 8   *From PKI to the Comintern, 1924–1941: The Apprenticeship of the Malayan Communist Party*, Cheah Boon Kheng. 1992. 147 pp. ISBN 0-87727-125-9

Number 7   *Intellectual Property and US Relations with Indonesia, Malaysia, Singapore, and Thailand*, Elisabeth Uphoff. 1991. 67 pp. ISBN 0-87727-124-0

Number 6   *The Rise and Fall of the Communist Party of Burma (CPB)*, Bertil Lintner. 1990. 124 pp. 26 illus., 14 maps. ISBN 0-87727-123-2

Number 5　　*Japanese Relations with Vietnam: 1951–1987*, Masaya Shiraishi. 1990. 174 pp. ISBN 0-87727-122-4

Number 3　　*Postwar Vietnam: Dilemmas in Socialist Development*, ed. Christine White, David Marr. 1988. 2nd printing 1993. 260 pp. ISBN 0-87727-120-8

Number 2　　*The Dobama Movement in Burma (1930–1938)*, Khin Yi. 1988. 160 pp. ISBN 0-87727-118-6

Translation Series

Volume 4　　*Approaching Suharto's Indonesia from the Margins*, ed. Takashi Shiraishi. 1994. 153 pp. ISBN 0-87727-403-7

Volume 3　　*The Japanese in Colonial Southeast Asia*, ed. Saya Shiraishi, Takashi Shiraishi. 1993. 172 pp. ISBN 0-87727-402-9

Volume 2　　*Indochina in the 1940s and 1950s*, ed. Takashi Shiraishi, Motoo Furuta. 1992. 196 pp. ISBN 0-87727-401-0

Volume 1　　*Reading Southeast Asia*, ed. Takashi Shiraishi. 1990. 188 pp. ISBN 0-87727-400-2

CORNELL MODERN INDONESIA PROJECT PUBLICATIONS

Cornell University

Number 75　　*A Tour of Duty: Changing Patterns of Military Politics in Indonesia in the 1990s*. Douglas Kammen and Siddharth Chandra. 1999. 99 pp. ISBN 0-87763-049-6

Number 74　　*The Roots of Acehnese Rebellion 1989–1992*, Tim Kell. 1995. 103 pp. ISBN 0-87763-040-2

Number 73　　*"White Book" on the 1992 General Election in Indonesia*, trans. Dwight King. 1994. 72 pp. ISBN 0-87763-039-9

Number 72　　*Popular Indonesian Literature of the Qur'an*, Howard M. Federspiel. 1994. 170 pp. ISBN 0-87763-038-0

Number 71　　*A Javanese Memoir of Sumatra, 1945–1946: Love and Hatred in the Liberation War*, Takao Fusayama. 1993. 150 pp. ISBN 0-87763-037-2

Number 70　　*East Kalimantan: The Decline of a Commercial Aristocracy*, Burhan Magenda. 1991. 120 pp. ISBN 0-87763-036-4

Number 69　　*The Road to Madiun: The Indonesian Communist Uprising of 1948*, Elizabeth Ann Swift. 1989. 120 pp. ISBN 0-87763-035-6

Number 68　　*Intellectuals and Nationalism in Indonesia: A Study of the Following Recruited by Sutan Sjahrir in Occupation Jakarta*, J. D. Legge. 1988. 159 pp. ISBN 0-87763-034-8

Number 67　　*Indonesia Free: A Biography of Mohammad Hatta*, Mavis Rose. 1987. 252 pp. ISBN 0-87763-033-X

Number 66　　*Prisoners at Kota Cane*, Leon Salim, trans. Audrey Kahin. 1986. 112 pp. ISBN 0-87763-032-1

Number 65　　*The Kenpeitai in Java and Sumatra*, trans. Barbara G. Shimer, Guy Hobbs, intro. Theodore Friend. 1986. 80 pp. ISBN 0-87763-031-3

Number 64 *Suharto and His Generals: Indonesia's Military Politics, 1975–1983*, David Jenkins. 1984. 4th printing 1997. 300 pp. ISBN 0-87763-030-5

Number 62 *Interpreting Indonesian Politics: Thirteen Contributions to the Debate, 1964–1981,* ed. Benedict Anderson, Audrey Kahin, intro. Daniel S. Lev. 1982. 3rd printing 1991. 172 pp. ISBN 0-87763-028-3

Number 61 *Sickle and Crescent: The Communist Revolt of 1926 in Banten*, Michael C. Williams. 1982. 81 pp. ISBN 0-87763-027-5

Number 60 *The Minangkabau Response to Dutch Colonial Rule in the Nineteenth Century*, Elizabeth E. Graves. 1981. 157 pp. ISBN 0-87763-000-3

Number 59 *Breaking the Chains of Oppression of the Indonesian People: Defense Statement at His Trial on Charges of Insulting the Head of State, Bandung, June 7–10, 1979*, Heri Akhmadi. 1981. 201 pp. ISBN 0-87763-001-1

Number 58 *Administration of Islam in Indonesia*, Deliar Noer. 1978. 82 pp. ISBN 0-87763-002-X

Number 57 *Permesta: Half a Rebellion*, Barbara S. Harvey. 1977. 174 pp. ISBN 0-87763-003-8

Number 55 *Report from Banaran: The Story of the Experiences of a Soldier during the War of Independence*, Maj. Gen. T. B. Simatupang. 1972. 186 pp. ISBN 0-87763-005-4

Number 52 *A Preliminary Analysis of the October 1 1965, Coup in Indonesia (Prepared in January 1966)*, Benedict R. Anderson, Ruth T. McVey, assist. Frederick P. Bunnell. 1971. 3rd printing 1990. 174 pp. ISBN 0-87763-008-9

Number 51 *The Putera Reports: Problems in Indonesian-Japanese War-Time Cooperation*, Mohammad Hatta, trans., intro. William H. Frederick. 1971. 114 pp. ISBN 0-87763-009-7

Number 50 *Schools and Politics: The Kaum Muda Movement in West Sumatra (1927–1933)*, Taufik Abdullah. 1971. 257 pp. ISBN 0-87763-010-0

Number 49 *The Foundation of the Partai Muslimin Indonesia*, K. E. Ward. 1970. 75 pp. ISBN 0-87763-011-9

Number 48 *Nationalism, Islam and Marxism*, Soekarno, intro. Ruth T. McVey. 1970. 2nd printing 1984. 62 pp. ISBN 0-87763-012-7

Number 43 *State and Statecraft in Old Java: A Study of the Later Mataram Period, 16th to 19th Century*, Soemarsaid Moertono. Revised edition 1981. 180 pp. ISBN 0-87763-017-8

Number 37 *Mythology and the Tolerance of the Javanese*, Benedict R. O'G. Anderson. 2nd edition 1997. 104 pp., 65 illus. ISBN 0-87763-041-0

Number 25 *The Communist Uprisings of 1926–1927 in Indonesia: Key Documents*, ed., intro. Harry J. Benda, Ruth T. McVey. 1960. 2nd printing 1969. 177 pp. ISBN 0-87763-024-0

Number 7 *The Soviet View of the Indonesian Revolution*, Ruth T. McVey. 1957. 3rd printing 1969. 90 pp. ISBN 0-87763-018-6

Number 6 *The Indonesian Elections of 1955*, Herbert Feith. 1957. 2nd printing 1971. 91 pp. ISBN 0-87763-020-8

LANGUAGE TEXTS

INDONESIAN

Beginning Indonesian Through Self-Instruction, John U. Wolff, Dédé Oetomo, Daniel Fietkiewicz. 3rd revised edition 1992. 3 volume set. 1,057 pp. ISBN 0-87727-519-X

Indonesian Readings, John U. Wolff. 1978. 4th printing 1992. 480 pp. ISBN 0-87727-517-3

Indonesian Conversations, John U. Wolff. 1978. 3rd printing 1991. 297 pp. ISBN 0-87727-516-5

Formal Indonesian, John U. Wolff. 2nd revised edition 1986. 446 pp. ISBN 0-87727-515-7

TAGALOG

Pilipino Through Self-Instruction, John U. Wolff, Ma. Theresa C. Centano, Der-Hwa U. Rau. 1991. 4 volume set. 1,490 pp. ISBN 0-87727-524-6

THAI

A. U. A. Language Center Thai Course Book 1, J. Marvin Brown. Originally published by the American University Alumni Association Language Center, 1974. Reissued by Cornell Southeast Asia Program,1991. 267 pp. ISBN 0-87727-506-8

A. U. A. Language Center Thai Course Book 2, 1992. 288 pp. ISBN 0-87727-507-6

A. U. A. Language Center Thai Course Book 3, 1992. 247 pp. ISBN 0-87727-508-4

A. U. A. Language Center Thai Course, Reading and Writing Text (mostly reading), 1979. Reissued 1997. 164 pp. ISBN 0-87727-511-4

A. U. A. Language Center Thai Course, Reading and Writing Workbook (mostly writing), 1979. Reissued 1997. 99 pp. ISBN 0-87727-512-2

KHMER

Cambodian System of Writing and Beginning Reader, Franklin E. Huffman. Originally published by Yale University Press, 1970. Reissued by Cornell Southeast Asia Program, 3rd printing 1992. 365 pp. ISBN 0-300-01314-0

Modern Spoken Cambodian, Franklin E. Huffman, assist. Charan Promchan, Chhom-Rak Thong Lambert. Originally published by Yale University Press, 1970. Reissued by Cornell Southeast Asia Program, 3rd printing 1991. 451 pp. ISBN 0-300-01316-7

Intermediate Cambodian Reader, ed. Franklin E. Huffman, assist. Im Proum. Originally published by Yale University Press, 1972. Reissued by Cornell Southeast Asia Program, 1988. 499 pp. ISBN 0-300-01552-6

Cambodian Literaru Reader and Glossary, Franklin E. Huffman, Im Proum. Originally published by Yale University Press, 1977. Reissued by Cornell Southeast Asia Program, 1988. 494 pp. ISBN 0-300-02069-4

HMONG

White Hmong-English Dictionary, Ernest E. Heimbach. 1969. 7th printing 1997. 523 pp. ISBN 0-87727-075-9

VIETNAMESE

Intermediate Spoken Vietnamese, Franklin E. Huffman, Tran Trong Hai. 1980. 3rd printing 1994. ISBN 0-87727-500-9

* * *

Southeast Asian Studies: Reorientations. Craig J. Reynolds and Ruth McVey. Frank H. Golay Lectures 2 & 3. 70 pp. ISBN 0-87727-301-4

Javanese Literature in Surakarta Manuscripts, Nancy K. Florida. Hard cover series ISBN 0-87727-600-5; Paperback series ISBN 0-87727-601-3. Vol. 1, *Introduction and Manuscripts of the Karaton Surakarta*. 1993. 410 pp. Frontispiece, 5 illus. Hard cover, ISBN 0-87727-602-1, Paperback, ISBN 0-87727-603-X

Sbek Thom: Khmer Shadow Theater. Pech Tum Kravel, trans. Sos Kem, ed. Thavro Phim, Sos Kem, Martin Hatch. 1996. 363 pp., 153 photographs. ISBN 0-87727-620-X

In the Mirror, Literature and Politics in Siam in the American Era, ed. Benedict R. O'G. Anderson, trans. Benedict R. O'G. Anderson, Ruchira Mendiones. 1985. 2nd printing 1991. 303 pp. Paperback. ISBN 974-210-380-1

To order, please contact:

Cornell University
SEAP Distribution Center
369 Pine Tree Rd.
Ithaca, NY 14850-2819 USA

Tel: 1-877-865-2432 (Toll free – U.S.)
Fax: (607) 255-7534

E-mail: SEAP-Pubs@cornell.edu

Orders must be prepaid by check or credit card (VISA, MasterCard, Discover).

Lightning Source UK Ltd.
Milton Keynes UK
UKHW031833260719
346854UK00020B/820/P